A SAVIOR
Worth Having

A SAVIOR
Worth Having

E.V. HILL

This Billy Graham Library Selection special edition
is published by the Billy Graham Evangelistic Association
with permission from Moody Press.

MOODY PRESS
CHICAGO

All Scripture quotations unless indicated are taken from the Holy Bible: King James
Version.

Scripture quotations marked NASB are taken from the *New American Standard Bible,* ©
1960, 1962, 1963, 1968, 1971, 1972, 1973, 1975, and 1977, the Lockman Founda-
tion, La Habra, Calif. Used by permission.

Editorial services by:
Julie-Allyson Ieron, Joy Media

Grateful acknowledgment is hereby expressed to those who have granted permission to
include copyrighted materials in this book. Any inadvertent omission of credit will be
gladly corrected in future editions.

Library of Congress Cataloging-in-Publication Data

Hill, E. V. (Edward Victor), 1933–2003
   A Savior worth having / E. V. Hill
     p. cm.
   ISBN 1-59328-003-3
   Previous ISBN 0-8024-3132-1
   1. Baptists—Sermons. 2. Sermons, American—20th century. I. Title.

A **Billy Graham Library Selection** designates materials that are appropriate
to a well-rounded collection of quality Christian literature, including both
classic and contemporary reading and reference materials.

Printed in the United States of America

This book is dedicated to my wife and family and the Mt. Zion Missionary Baptist Church for all of their support.
Special thanks to Joe Mines, Wendell St. Clair, Greg Thornton and all the Moody Press staff for helping to bring this book together.

CONTENTS

PREFACE

I have had a blessed life, thanks to this amazing Savior you are about to read about. It hasn't always been an easy life. It hasn't all been smooth sailing. But my Savior has walked with me through every day, ever since I met Him way back when I was eleven in a little place called Sweet Home Community in rural Texas. Since that day I've enjoyed His blessings. He has given me so much, and I want to tell you all about what He's done for me.

If you don't know Him, you should. And you can. Just read on.

In these pages you'll find a collection of sermons that I've delivered over the years. They all center around this wonderful Savior, Jesus. And together they all paint a picture of our glorious Lord.

I believe you'll find this book easy to read and easy to understand. But, I'd ask you not to try to read it all in one sitting. Instead, as you read one chapter at a time, take a few moments to reflect on the truths you've read. You'll get the most out of it if you stop frequently and consider your own journey as you read about mine.

So, as I invite you to listen to my story of my journey with Jesus, I'd like you to reflect on a very special truth. It comes from the lips of this loving Savior, spoken to a crowd of people 2000 years ago. It is, in fact, an invitation to know Him as your own Savior, One who offers rest and peace and comfort:

Come unto me, all ye that labor and are heavy laden,
and I will give you rest. Take my yoke upon you,
and learn of me; for I am meek and lowly in heart,
and ye shall find rest unto your souls.
For my yoke is easy, and my burden is light.
(Matthew 11:28–30)

FOREWORD

We sat spellbound as Dr. E. V. Hill tossed books, one after the other, out into the waiting congregation of students, faculty, and staff. In his inimitable, powerful preaching style he punctuated the words of his sermon with this picture lesson of how Christ bestows unexpected blessings on His children. "He often just says, 'Here! Take this!'—and He blesses us again and again, not because of our faithfulness, but because He is the Supreme Giver."

Well, needless to say, this message entitled "What Do You Have When You Have Jesus?" has gone down in the annals of Moody Bible Institute Founders

Week history as one of the most memorable, challenging and classic messages of all time. *A Savior Worth Having* includes this message and many others. Dr. Hill argues without apology that our Savior is above all others, He is Supreme, all-sufficient, a restorer of the soul, and singularly able to save.

What a joy it is to know that—in these tumultuous, changing times—when standards are changing as quickly as they are established—there is One who changes not! I enthusiastically concur with Dr. Hill that our Christ is undeniably *A Savior Worth Having!*

Dr. Joseph Stowell

Chapter One

NO OTHER NAME

*"And when they had set them in the midst, they asked,
By what power or by what name, have ye done this?"* —Acts 4:7

*"Be it known unto you all, and to all the people of Israel,
that by the name of Jesus Christ of Nazareth,
whom ye crucified, whom God raised from the dead,
even by him doth this man stand here before you well."* —Acts 4:10

*"Neither is there salvation in any other; for there is
no other name under heaven given among men,
whereby we must be saved."* —Acts 4:12

What's in a name?

Of all the names on earth today, one name is more powerful than any other. Christians know it has the power to change lives, save lost souls, heal sick bodies, and secure eternity. It is the name of our beloved Savior, Jesus.

I was reared in a log cabin; Momma and I came up together. Papa passed on when I was eleven. Momma and I battled through. Then Momma passed on, and every so often when I am privileged to speak in one of the great venues of Christendom,

I ask the Lord, "Lord, let Momma see me here!" (I realize theologically it's not quite possible—but I didn't go to seminary, so I can take this liberty.)

WHEREVER YOU GO,
NO MATTER WHAT CLASS—
WHETHER IT'S POLITICIANS,
SEMINARIANS, PROFESSORS,
TEACHERS, OR EVEN WITH
PEOPLE WHOSE HOMES
ARE BREAKING UP—
THE HEART'S PLEA IS,
"I NEED A SAVIOR."

One of the great thrills of my life was preaching in Moscow several years ago—just a couple of blocks from Lenin's Tomb, in the heart of Moscow. I was speaking to about 6,000 preachers (I suspect old Lenin was turning over in his grave) about this wonderful Jesus. For now, even in Moscow, the name of Jesus can be publicly spoken. Who would have thought four or five or ten years ago that the name "Jesus" could be uttered freely on the streets of the former Soviet Union? Tragically, while in Russian public schools He can be read about and discussed freely, in our own public schools, it is forbidden to speak His name.

WHO NEEDS A SAVIOR?

Wherever you go, no matter what class—whether it's politicians, seminarians, professors, teachers, or even with people whose homes are breaking up—the heart's plea is, "I need a savior." Even the brightest minds need a savior.

One of the members of the Mount Zion church where I pastor, holds a double master's degree in Law and Finance. He left my church and went to another group that dealt with the mind, for he said he wanted to go to a place that fed his mind. He complained that the average preacher was too simple in his presentation, that he needed someone who would deal with his mind.

So I told him, "I'll be praying for you." Then I added, "Incidentally, you are not my attorney anymore."

He replied, "Why? Are you prejudiced because I'm leaving your church?"

Then I said, "No, I just don't want an attorney who doesn't know the difference between stepping up and falling down."

Then one Sunday I was preaching my National Children's Day sermon. And I was speaking on Billy (my rabbit). Billy was a wonderful rabbit, and I was telling the children about Billy. At invitation time, here comes this double-master fellow down the aisle.

He says, "Pastor, that's the greatest sermon I've ever heard you preach!" Even someone with a double master's degree needs a savior.

Some of the most obstinate and argumentative youth today are now saying, "I need a savior." The most critical minds are now agreeing that things are out of order, that things are topsy-turvy. Even the most brilliant minds, who seem to have so much confidence in their own ability, are now saying, "I need a savior." In fact, at one point or another everyone asks, "Who can save me?" They are beyond the point of handling life on their own, and they finally admit, "I need a savior."

A SAVIOR IS NOT . . .

While people who do not believe in God (or so they say) may be coming to the conclusion that they need a savior, they're still searching. They acknowledge that somebody needs to rescue them, but they do not recognize the true rescuer.

One of the things many are pointing out is that we know what a savior is not. We know that it's not silver and gold, houses and lands. We know that it's not because people with silver and gold, houses and lands, too, are saying, "We need a savior." In fact, they're saying, "I need a savior, someone to rescue me. I have silver and gold, houses and lands, but I'm not secure. I'm trembling within. I fear the future. I now realize I cannot buy the future. I need somebody to walk with through the dark paths."

Now I want to discuss this matter of having the best savior. Since you have to have one, why not the best one? I'm not suggesting that there are plenty of *saviors,* I know that there is only one; that's Jesus. But being ignorant of God's righteousness, men have gone about to establish a smorgasbord of so-called saviors. And those have many followers.

But why not the best one? Why not test those who say they are the savior? Why not examine them, put them on trial, since it involves our happiness now, and our eternal life with God? Why not test him, her, or whomever you have put your faith in? It makes good sense; since you are going to pick one, why not the best?

The text in Acts 4 addresses this discussion. A great miracle has happened in the healing of a disabled man. Then the question comes up, "How did you do this? By what power did this happen? How is it that this man is healed and standing before us? In whose name was this miracle performed? Who did you call, what mayor, governor, or authority—whose name did you use?"

Then Peter rose up and said, "Now to be truthful with you, there is only one name that can perform a miracle such as this. That name is Jesus!" Someone with the kind of power that can heal a disabled man, that's the kind of Savior we all need.

QUALIFICATIONS OF A SAVIOR

If we want to pick the best savior, first of all, he ought to be old enough. I'm over sixty, and I have to have somebody who was here before I got here. I can't trust anyone who is in his forties or fifties.

I have to have someone who was available to Momma, and to Momma's momma. I have to have someone who was in control—someone who was a part of the beginning, in fact, who was the beginning. I can't trust these youngsters who, just because they look strange and act peculiar, suggest they can save me, help me, and get me over. I need a Savior older than this generation. One who was before the beginning. One by whom everything that was made was made and without whom nothing was made. One who was not a graduate of seminary, not a graduate of philosophy, not a follower of some teacher, not someone who came out of nowhere and did something mystic and strange and now asks me to follow him as a savior.

I need somebody who is acquainted with all the generations and with all of time. I need somebody who can deal with all the aspects of living and learning. I need somebody who knows how to deal with the brokenhearted. I need somebody who knows how to speak to me in the lonely hours. I need somebody to give me instruction when I need to be instructed. Someone who knows how to instruct, who's not guessing and who doesn't have to read a book himself, for He Himself *is* the book. That's who I need. I don't need somebody who takes my problems and rushes to the library for answers. I need somebody who *is* the library. I need somebody who can stand up and talk to my spirit as the author and finisher of my faith. That's what I need when I talk about a savior. I don't need anybody to go out and take a quick course in Greek and then come back and try to tell me how to get to heaven.

You're no different. You need somebody who already has prepared the road for you to take.

Next, I need a savior who will be everlasting. I don't want to get all tied up with someone, then the savior dies! It must be an awful thing to go to your savior's funeral. Elijah Mohammed boasted so much that he was the prophet sent from God. It must have been a sad day for his followers when thousands of young people in Chicago watched twelve young men pass his casket to the grave.

I don't want to get wrapped up in a man who beats me dying. I need somebody who can walk with me through the valley of the shadow of death myself. I need company in that time when I go through some place I've never been. I don't want somebody who will run out on me before I die.

A SAVIOR THROUGH LIFE'S TUNNELS

I was in Detroit and a friend of mine said, "Let's go over to Canada for dinner." He picked me up at the hotel. All of a sudden, he began to drive through the tunnel that leads from Detroit to Windsor, Canada. I suffer from claustrophobia, and I never shall forget. I yelled, "Stop! Stop!"

But the car was in the flow of traffic so he said, "I can't stop. What's the matter?"

I said, "I can't go through this tunnel. You'll have a dead man on your hands by the time you reach the other side."

He looked at me, and touched my hand, and said, "Hill, you'll be alright. See those folks in the other cars? They're alright."

But I said, "Stop the car. I'll get out and walk to the other side."

But he said, "You can't do that; you'll get hurt with all that traffic." To which I replied, it would be better to get hurt than to die. But he just kept on going and said, "Hold my hand, just hold on."

Now there'll come a time when I'll face another tunnel that I've never been through before. I'll need a savior who can say, "Hold my hand, we're almost through." I know someday someone will carry my casket, but my soul will be led by a hand that's everlasting and will walk me through the valley of the shadow of death. Someone whose hand will be steady and who will say, "Hill, you'll be alright."

Before you pick a savior, before you decide in whom you'll put your faith, you need to check out his track record. Who else has he saved? Who else's life has he changed? Who else's tears has he wiped away? Has he picked up the heavyhearted or walked through the stormy seas with anyone else? Who else can testify that this Jesus of Nazareth, whom God raised from the dead, has the name by which a man has been made whole? Who else gave sight to the blind? Who else told Lazarus to come forth? Who else has turned around at His name, drug addicts, pimps, prostitutes, and alcoholics? Who has rescued men from crime? It's not good enough that He is everlasting, but you need Him to have a track record of successfully saving others.

Jesus saves! Aha. He has a track record. He addresses the most difficult tasks head-on. He changes water into wine. He walks on water, and seas behave at His command. Who else can just speak a word, and at His word a child be made whole? Who else dies on a rugged cross and the sun ceases to shine? Who else is put in a grave and arrives in hell to preach to the spirits, then arrives back in the grave only to walk out on Sunday morning with all power in His hands? That was two thousand years ago, but who else still lives, still saves, still mends wounded and broken hearts, still turns people's lives around?

There are tens of thousands of witnesses down through the ages who can testify to the healing, converting, life-changing power of this Savior. By Him these miracles have been wrought. By His name this man so long ago was healed. There is no other name under heaven by which we must be saved. I join Peter in telling you without a doubt, "There is no other name!"

COMPLETELY TRUSTWORTHY

I've had the privilege of meeting with six presidents of the United States. But these are just men; they come and they go. But this Jesus I offer to you is the Savior in whom you can put your complete trust.

I believe this little verse written by C. Austin Miles (1868– 1946) and sung as the sacred hymn "In the Garden" explains the relationship I have with my Savior:

> *I come to the garden alone*
> *while the dew is still on the roses.*
> *And the voice I hear falling on my ear*
> *The Son of God discloses.*

And He walks with me and He talks with me
And He tells me I am His own.
And the joy we share as we tarry there
None other has ever known.

I don't own the best house in Los Angeles. I don't have the finest car in Los Angeles. I don't have a mint of money. I don't even have the largest church in Los Angeles. But I do have the best Savior.

You who are reading this book, right now, if you haven't done so already, you need to pick the best, the one about whom others testify. Rich or poor, white or black, there's one thing we can all have . . . the same Savior. As I said before, now I repeat, there is no other name under heaven, given among men, whereby we must be saved. His name is Jesus.

Chapter Two

IN THE
NAME OF JESUS

"Then Peter said, 'Silver and gold have I none;
but, such as I have, give I thee.
In the name of Jesus Christ of Nazareth,
rise up and walk.'" —*Acts 3:6*

I buy all my suits on Jewish row in Chicago. I buy the best suits that way. On Jewish row I pay $100 to buy the same suits they sell at Neiman Marcus for $400. I have people admiring these suits all the time. Once I bought a suit worth $650, but it had a small moth hole on the lapel, so I paid $100 for it. Every Sunday I covered that hole with a carnation. You have to be on the ball to survive in the big city.

I don't have a problem with that. If you're going to buy clothing, you try to buy a suit or dress that is worth having. If you're going to spend money on buying a car, you try to buy one that is worth having.

Even when it comes to choosing a wife, you want to choose one worth having. In fact, I've chosen two. Baby, my first wife, is in Glory, and the other one is in Los Angeles. That's far enough apart so they don't fight, they don't argue. As a matter of fact, the one I have now admires the other one very much. She knew her and admired her. Now, when I have rainy seasons about Baby (and I still do from time to time), my wife is a classy lady; she just walks out of the room and lets me have my quiet time alone.

Anyway, when I was picking my second wife, I wanted one worth having. If we're so careful about picking furniture, or cars, or even mates—which is as it should be—then, why not have a savior worth having? I don't want a savior who has eyes and can't see, who has hands and can't lift, who has feet and can't walk. I need a savior who does walk, who does talk, who can reach, who can lift. I have that Savior in Jesus Christ. Nothing else or nobody else is qualified to be my savior.

THAT SAVIOR'S NAME

Let us take a closer look at the third and fourth chapters of the book of Acts, which we discussed briefly last chapter. These Scriptures reveal that there was a lame man sitting at the temple gate begging alms. When Peter and John were going up to the temple to pray, they saw him. They felt compassion on him and called on Jesus' name to heal him. This caused a miraculous thing to happen: The lame man immediately received new strength in his legs and went leaping and shouting and praising God into the temple along with them.

This occasion caused quite a stir among the rulers and the leaders of Israel, because thousands of people began to discuss this miraculous happening. Of course that even affected the attendance at the synagogue. There were thousands accepting Christ as a result of this miracle.

This also caused a turmoil among the nation's leaders. They began debating about what they should do, how they should react. They realized they could not deny that a great miracle had happened, because the man was there for all to see and hear. They couldn't dispute this evidence; it was indisputable. Here was this man who used to be lame and used to lie begging alms at the temple gate. Now, all at once he was leaping for joy, praising God, and causing great havoc. The religious leadership was now inquiring by what power and in whose name this thing had happened.

Peter, the great spokesman, replied, "In the name of Jesus. This is done in the name of Jesus." More and more, we who are born again should give credit to the *name* of Jesus.

Often, when people are sick or down and out,

when they are out of a job and don't have any money, so often they say, "The Lord is the one on whom I'm leaning and trusting." But as soon as things turn around, they say, "You know I've been smart all my life, I've known all my life how to work things out." But that's not true. You ought to give credit to whom credit is due.

That's what Peter and John did. They said, "It is the name of Jesus—this is done in the name of the Savior, Jesus. He is responsible for this miracle." That is why I say to you, it is so important that you pick a savior who is worth having.

DON'T USE THE NAME

These rulers went on to say, "We know that a great miracle has happened, but we can't have this happening here—all these five thousand men following Jesus Christ. We've got to do something." Somebody came up with a brilliant idea. They said, "Call those two people in. They know we are the rulers; they know that we are the elders of Israel, so call them in and let's threaten them real good." They said, "We'll tell them that they've performed a great miracle, and all that, but that isn't the kind of preaching we want in our town, and that's not the kind of results we want people all wrought up about."

"Our threat will let them understand that we

don't want anything like that done in *that* name anymore. That name is disturbing the city. That name is causing things to happen that we can't duplicate. That name is causing men who've never walked before to walk. That name is upsetting the city." And that name continues to upset the city. It should upset the city, for He is the worthy one. This name, *Jesus,* it will upset things, it will turn things that are upside down to the upright position.

So they told the disciples, "You can preach, but not in the name of Jesus. Because we have seen evidence that that is an authentic name. We've had other men come in and do hocus pocus, throw sheets over people, and anoint them, but nothing happened." The devil doesn't object to those counterfeits. He says, come on in and do your act. Charge $10, get in a faith line, and I'll perform my trick. The devil doesn't mind that, but when he sees an authentic testimony, that's different. This man is standing here, no argument—he's standing here, walking and leaping, completely healed. He's an authentic testament.

I might add, it not only includes the physical lameness, but it also includes the man or woman, boy or girl, who has had an authentic change of life and faith. One who formerly did not know the Lord but does now in a truly personal way. It certainly includes an authentic witness against Satan and proves that Satan is against him.

Now we can take a clue from that. The devil has not changed his *modus operandi*. He has not altered his procedure, for even today the devil believes that if he just threatens the church, if he just threatens the preacher, if he just threatens the Christian, he can stop the message from reaching the lost. The devil still believes he can stop the church by calling it in and threatening it. He says, let's threaten them by the laws, by the Internal Revenue Service, by *every* means possible. Then they'll keep quiet. He has the idea that the church can be quieted by these means. Especially be quieted in our approach to reach lost men and women with the gospel.

Even now in some of our cemet . . . I mean in our seminaries, they aren't talking about this name enough. Some of them are even denying this name. You can visit some of those universities on the East Coast (I won't name them, but you know that bunch up there) and they never even call on the name of Jesus. Besides that, there are people who publish great books and ignore the name of Jesus. In fact, the year before last they awarded the outstanding sermon of the year, and it never mentioned Jesus' name!

How can you preach a sermon without Jesus? He's the subject and the center. He's the introduction, He's the argument, and He's the conclusion. How can you preach a sermon without Jesus? There are a lot of needs in my community and yours, but the greatest need is that people need to know Jesus, because, when He is known, things begin to come to order.

A POWERFUL RESPONSE

When they called Peter and John in they said, "We want to talk to you. Now we know that you have a powerful name there. You've been using it, and there was a great miracle. We're not here to dispute that. But we are here to say that we can't handle that here in this town. The rulers and elders of Israel have gotten together and decided that you can't preach in that name anymore. If you do not comply, we'll have to take severe action against you. Just take our warning, be good boys and go on home, and nothing further will happen to you."

Then Peter spoke up and said, "You'll have to judge whether or not we should obey you or obey God. But as for us, we have a condition, and it's contagious and it's called 'can't-help-it.' We couldn't stop if we wanted to. We could not stop in spite of your threats. We are not spectators; we are participators. No matter how you have threatened us and forbidden us to preach by this name, we will continue to do it, because we can't help it. This isn't something we can cut on and off."

It's just like I explained to my wife, before we got married: We're not going to cut this on and off. You'll not be lovely to me in the morning, and ugly at night. You just have to let the sweetness flow.

Peter and John said, "You have to do what you have to do, and we have to do what we have to do. But we have the 'can't-help-it.' It's all over us. We can't help it because of what we have seen and what we have heard. We're not just out here shouting— we've seen something and we've heard something, and based on what we have seen and what we have heard, we must talk about it.

"We were with Jesus when He turned the water into wine. We were right there with Him when He hollered to Lazarus to come forth, and he came walking out as if he had never been dead. We were there when He gave sight to the blind. Don't tell us to shut up; we've got evidence." They said that on that basis they were going to keep on preaching Jesus. "We can't help it," they proclaimed.

DESPITE THE ENEMY'S THREATS

I've seen something! I can't stop! The church today needs a great dose of "can't-help-it." It's got to be, even if you are threatened, you can't help it. I was threatened by the Ku Klux Klan and told by them that I had six weeks to live. I was only twenty-five years old then; I'm over sixty-one now and still preaching. All because I can't help it! That's what I told the Ku Klux Klan. "I'm on my way to the land of integration and opportunity. Do what you have to do, but you won't stop me."

I WANT TO TALK ABOUT THIS GREAT CHRIST THE MIGHTY SAVIOR. I WANT TO NAME HIM JESUS, AND I WANT TO CALL HIS NAME OUT LOUD! SO IF IT'S MY LAST TIME, AND A BULLET STRIKES ME DOWN, I WANT TO GO OUT SAYING, *JESUS!*

The Black Panthers said I had one day to live. That was on a Tuesday. They said if I preached about this white Jesus one more time they'd be there and blow my brains out. That Tuesday my office was in a turmoil—that is, everyone but my wife. She said the Lord had delivered me so many times He wasn't going to let me down this time. The Panthers said they would be there on Sunday, and they ordered me to preach on *blackness* and not this white Christ. I said, I don't know anything about a white Christ—I know about Christ, a Savior, named Jesus! I don't know what color He is. He was born in brown Asia,

He fled to black Africa, and He was in heaven before the gospel got to white Europe, so I don't know what color He is. I do know one thing, if you bow at the altar with color on your mind, and get up with color on your mind, go back again—and keep going back until you no longer look at His color, but at His greatness and His power—His power to save!

So I was threatened by these Panthers. The policemen came. They inspected the church and then they said, "Now pastor, on Sunday you can't preach."

I said, "Oh no. As a matter of fact I wish it were Sunday now. I've got this message on my heart now (this was Wednesday) and it's burning." Then I said, "It's your job to keep me living, and it's my job to keep on preaching."

On that Sunday my deacons came and said, "We'll all sit in the front row."

I said, "Sit wherever you want. I've got my message. I want to talk about this great Christ the mighty Savior. I want to name Him Jesus, and I want to call His name out loud! So if it's my last time, and a bullet strikes me down, I want to go out saying, *Jesus!*"

By the way, one of the reasons we should come to church is so that the world can see and testify that we have accepted Christ as our Savior. We must not stand off from the church, but be with the church, with the pastor, with the administration. Like these deacons, we need to identify with the church in good times and bad. We need to be glad to tell people, "I'm going to church. I may or may not see the ball game, but I'm going to church."

So, I told the Black Panther party, "The One you say I can't preach about has brought me too far. Now do what you have to do, but I've got to call His name!" I recall a great lyric written by W. C. Martin back in 1901 titled "The Name of Jesus," that's as true today as it was more than 100 years ago:

> *Jesus, O how sweet the name.*
> *Jesus, ev'ry day the same,*
> *Jesus, let all saints proclaim*
> *His worthy praise, forever.*

So I join Peter and John. Don't ask me not to speak His name. I've seen too much, I've been through too much, and God has brought me a mighty long way. And as long as I have breath, I live to tell about it. The anonymous gospel song "Never Alone" says it so well:

> *I've seen the lightning flashing,*
> *And heard the thunder roll,*
> *I've felt sins' breakers dashing*
> *Trying to conquer my soul,*

But I've heard the voice of my Saviour,
Telling me still to fight on.
He promised never to leave me,
Never to leave me alone.

To this day, I rely totally on that blessed name, the name of *Jesus!*

Chapter Three

HOW TO PICK A SAVIOR

"Choose you this day whom ye will serve."
—Joshua 24:15

We inevitably seek something or someone to serve. Some of the available choices are shocking. There are men who worship cars and consider them to be holy. In India there are people who would starve to death rather than eat beef, because to them cattle are sacred. There are people who worship the sun, moon, and stars. There are those who worship almost anything: snakes, fowl, etc. They submit themselves to these creatures as their master.

San Francisco is increasingly becoming a town of idolatry. In San Francisco not only can you find all kinds of major religions, but you can find all sorts of minor ones. The latest being a church that is organized and taking in members around the music of a blues singer. He is now their messiah. They claim his songs have salvation in them. They play his records and worship at his picture.

Man inevitably will seek a master. That's what's behind men who give women all their earnings, because they want to be mastered. That's what's behind a prostitute who will give a pimp all her money: She seeks to be mastered. People are instinctively seeking a messiah, a master, a god. Being ignorant of God's righteousness, they've gone about to establish their own righteousness. They have not submitted themselves to the righteousness of God. It is truly a critical situation that calls for an awakening.

> THE GOSPEL HAS ALL HOPE IN
> IT. IT IS MADE EVEN SWEETER
> BECAUSE IT IS A GIFT GIVEN
> TO US WITHOUT PRICE.
> YOU CAN COME AS YOU ARE.

I might also add that there is a new god on the horizon. It is the god of dope. It's sweeping the nation. I was watching a television show, recently, that was demonstrating how much of a control dope has on us today. And though men are strung out on this powerful god, seemingly helpless, they are not totally so, for God can break the chain of that worship and give freedom if help is sought. Unquestionably, dope is sorcery; dope is witchcraft; dope is a part of the entire demonic family. That is the reason you find so many weird signs, writings, and paintings from people who are on dope. Some of the pictures you see on rock albums are actually satanic pictures. Some of them look like the description of the harlot in the book of Revelation. Without question, there ain't no hope in dope.

I heard a preacher say he sniffed cocaine. He said it cleared his mind to preach. But I had one question for him: "Preach what?" Instead of going into the closet praying for power, he was in the closet sniffing cocaine.

If there ain't no hope in dope, where is the hope?

Born-again people have heard something full of great hope. The gospel has all hope in it. It is made even sweeter because it is a gift given to us without price. You can come as you are. Born-again people have heard the message of God that has guided them through the dark hours and days of life. Born-again people have heard the gospel story that has set their souls on fire when their hearts were bleeding within —they've heard something.

And I testify that I have heard something.

THE GOOD NEWS I HEARD

I was born in poverty in Columbus, Texas, seventy-five miles west on the San Antonio highway. My mother was a very poor woman, and when I was a year-and-a-half old my father left us. She moved with her four children to San Antonio, Texas. She got a job making $12.50 a week. Out of that had to come rent. Most of the food we had as children was leftovers from the white people's table where mother worked.

It was always a happy day when someone in that family was sick and didn't want to eat their steak. Mother would take that steak and that extra piece of chicken somebody didn't touch. Mother would take those leftover rolls and put them in a sack. If there wasn't enough meat of one kind, she would chop it all up together and make hash. Hash is still my favorite food.

I was born in poverty, but I heard something. I heard something. Even in my remote site in the country, I heard that Jesus loved me. It was in a little old country church that Rachel Anthony, God bless her heart, and Professor Esrey and Professor Arnold told me as a young boy, "God loves you, son. God has something in store for you and God will take care of you."

A Physical Hope

One day I was playing out in the yard when some elderly people came up and said, "Who is this boy who is so underfed?" I had a great big head and a distended stomach, from malnutrition.

Someone said, "That's Miss Hill's boy."

"Where is Miss Hill?"

"She's working."

"Who takes care of the children when she's gone?"

"They take care of themselves."

So they waited until mother came home. They said, "We're the Langdons. We live out in the country. Our sister lives next door to you. She's ill; we come up every two weeks to see her. All our children are grown and gone. We live alone, and we have plenty. We'd like to take this boy and girl (my sister) to the country where they could play." Then and there I heard the word *plenty*. It stuck in my ear. I had never been around a place where there was plenty.

My mother said, "Don't ask me to give my children away."

And they said, "Just drop us a line whenever you want them back, and we'll send them back to you right away."

The plenty turned out to be a two-room log cabin. I was looking for a great big old house. The plenty turned out to be wild rabbit, squirrel, hickory nuts, and wild berries.

An Emotional Hope

But I fell in love with Poppa, because I hadn't had a daddy who would caress me. There were no televisions, and we had to conserve the radio because it ran on battery. We listened to the news three times a day: eight in the morning, noon, and six at night, and one program. So Poppa had to entertain me on his knee. He told me stories about Brer Rabbit, and those kind of stories.

I've solved that problem myself by giving each of my children a TV in their own room. They can go in there and laugh about what they want to laugh about. But that wasn't the case in those days.

When I was six, my mother forced me to come back to San Antonio, so I could go to better schools. But I ran away, and after three days they found me. It was decided I could stay with the Langdons.

At age eleven I woke up one morning and found Poppa dead in his rocking chair. So from then until I was seventeen, Momma Langdon and I lived in that log cabin. In those days there was no check on the first and fifteenth, there were no social workers, and the only charities we ever got were apples, oranges, jelly, sugar, and cheese. But no checks. Momma and I had to pick cotton during the summer, and shake peanuts and pull corn. Sometimes we'd kill a hog and put it in the smokehouse, and get some syrup. That's how we lived in those days.

As for clothing, I had lots of hand-me-ups given to me. Just now and then did I have any boughten clothes. But I studied hard. Momma would drill into me every night, "You're poor and you're colored, but you can take but one ball and knock a home run."

One time when I had a fever of 105—and in my community no white doctor would see a Negro— the Negro doctor couldn't be found. Even if he were found, we wouldn't have the money to pay him. So my momma just put her hand on my forehead and said, "Lord, You know." That's all she said. The next morning I had to milk three cows and make four fires in my school before eight o'clock, and that fever was gone. All Momma had said was, "Lord, You know."

A Spiritual Hope

I never shall forget one time when it snowed and everything froze, and we ran out of food. I heard Momma praying. It was about midnight, for that was when she prayed. I heard her pray, "Lord, You know I have this boy, he's big and he eats, and he's hungry and we don't have no food. I can't get out, but You know all about it." The next morning at seven o'clock Bud Anthony rode by on his horse, pitched a whole sack of food on our porch, and kept on riding.

All Momma could say was, "Thank You, Lord." In fact, Momma was always praising the Lord. In church, she'd shout at least three times, "Yes!"

Now the devil has quieted the church in their "amens," in response to the preaching of the gospel. He seeks a quiet church, because even our amens back up the testimony of ourselves or somebody else. It's like one of the deacons I used to have in Texas. He said, "Pastor, the Lord am good." Now I didn't go too far in English, but I knew that wasn't right, so I said, "No, deacon, the Lord *is* good." He replied, "He sure am."

That reminds me of a Negro woman down South who was attending a white church. The white people were quiet and conservative. The pastor said, "Jesus is the Son of God."

She stood up and shouted, "Yes He is!" An usher came over to her and said, "I'm sorry, but we don't do that here."

She said, "But I got 'ligon, [religion]."

But he said, "You didn't get it here!"

She said, "I'll keep quiet."

Then the pastor said, "He died for our sins."

This lady said, "Yes He did!"

This time two ushers came over to her and said, "We're going to warn you just one more time. We're going to have to throw you out if you don't shut up. That's your culture, but we don't do that here."

So she said, "I'll try to hold my tongue."

And the preacher then said, "Early Sunday morning..."

She got up and shouted, "But He got up!!!" Two great big ushers came over and grabbed her and started to drag her out. All the while she shouted, "Praise the Lord!"

They said, "Why are you saying that?"

She said, "Well, Jesus rode in on one, and I'm ridin' out on two!"

Anyway, when I was in the ninth grade, Momma got up in prayer meeting and announced, "My boy is gonna finish high school." Well, in that community few Negro boys finished high school. Maybe you got to the tenth grade, but then you were hired out by a white farmer. The deacons cautioned her not to get too bigheaded. "That boy will finish tenth grade next year, and you can hire him out, as big as he is, for $2 a day to help you out." And she said, "He's gonna finish high school." And so I finished high school— president of my class, valedictorian, highest academic student in my class. By the way, I was the only student in my class.

But after my graduation my momma got up in prayer meeting and said, "My son's going to college."

That's when a committee of church rulers, deacons, etc., came over to Momma and said, "It's marvelous that your son finished high school, but this going to college thing... You need to let him go to work. He can get $3 a day now. You don't have any money; he doesn't have any money; we don't have any money; he can't go to no school."

Momma took me to the Trailway Bus station. Momma bought my ticket. She had got me a dark suit, a couple pairs of blue jeans and shirts. She wrapped a rope around my suitcase, and drew out five dollars from her purse, gave it to me, and said, "Now go on to school; the Lord will make a way." And just before I boarded the bus she said, "I'll be praying for you." I can still see her waving good-bye as the bus pulled out of the station.

I splurged on the way, and got to my destination with only $1.83 left. Then I had to pay a quarter to catch a bus down to the campus. I went straight to the registrar's office and got in line. The first thing I saw was a sign that said, "$83, cash, cashier's check or money order." And the devil said, "Now which one do you have?" Then I heard my momma saying, "I'll be praying for you." The devil said, "Don't be stupid; get out of line. This is no prayer meeting, no Sweet Home. With all due respects to your momma, she ain't in control now." And again, I heard my momma saying, "I'll be praying for you." So I just stayed in line and kept easing on up. I was one up when the devil said, "You're next. What are you going to do now with just $1.58?" But once again I heard Momma saying, "I'll be praying for you."

So with all my fearful misgivings, but with her

assurance, I moved on. I was just about to step up
when I felt a hand on my shoulder and Dr. Drew
said, "Are you Ed Hill?"

I said, "Yes, sir."

He said, "Get out of line." Here I had come all
this way just to be denied my place. But he said,
"Son, didn't you get our letter? We've been trying to
contact you. We are giving you a four-year scholarship. It will pay your tuition, room and board, and
give you $35 a month for spending money."

And once again I heard my momma say, "I'll be
praying for you."

I've heard something, and I've seen something.
I've seen both negative and positive. I've seen the
lightning flash, I've been through the rain and the
storm. I know what it is to suffer, to not have, to
want. I know what it is to be buffeted and scarred.
I've been through the grinding machine. I've seen
God open doors that no man could shut. I've seen
God work many miracles. So, this is the Master I
choose to serve.

CHOOSING A MASTER

We seek divine supplements. We know in ourselves we're not strong enough to resist evil. The
question is, who are you going to serve? That's why
Joshua said you've got to make up your mind:

"Choose you this day whom ye will serve" (Joshua 24:15). We need a master, we need a God, there's no question about it. And the truth is that if you don't choose one, an evil one will consume you.

It's impossible to remain neutral. If you don't select a power, a power will select you. If you don't take a stand, a stand will take you. You can't say, "I'm neither way." Someone once said to me, "Church is all right for those who need it." Well, I haven't run into anybody who doesn't need it. Those who think they don't need it, need it the most. So if you don't select a master, the evil one will consume you.

You don't, in yourself, have enough power to resist sin. Solomon didn't have enough, although he was a strong man. Samson didn't have enough, although he was a mighty strong man. David didn't have enough even though he was a strong man. When you try to operate without God's power, the power of evil will take over. Don't stick out your chest and say, "I'm in control." Many folks stronger than you have not been able to resist the power of Satan. You need a breastplate, you need a sword, and you need God to prevail.

A HEDGE OF PROTECTION

You remember Job, don't you? It was not Job's righteousness that put him where he was, it wasn't his strength that kept him, but God hedged him in. That's what you need to do every morning when you wake up—let God hedge you in. Though the devil is in the business of kicking down hedges, these are hedges that will withstand his onslaughts.

I saw a cartoon that said, "If anybody knows how to pray, pray now." In California they have prayers of all faiths take their turn to pray for the state. One day they'll have a Christian, the next a Jew, next a Buddhist, and so it goes. No wonder California is in such a state. Our leaders do this to accommodate man. This is not what our forefathers promised. They proclaimed, "In GOD we trust." Our founding documents did not say that this will be a country of many religions; they said that this would be a Christian nation.

I'd like to have a president who would remind this nation that it was founded to be a Christian nation. I would like to see a Congress that would open up in the name of Jesus! I'd like to see a people who would call on Jesus to solve their problems.

Problems will eventually become so intense that one of these nights you're going to crawl out of bed and call on somebody. Even the unbeliever, in the midst of a crisis, prays, "lord have mercy." The question is, what lord are you calling on? Ain't but one, and that's Jesus.

SOLD OUT TO WHOM?

There are many masters vying for your allegiance, particularly my young friends. Materialism would like to possess you. The militants would like to have you. Communism wants you. The Buddhists and other religions want you. The devil himself wants to control you. Jesus wants you. There's a large selection of saviors bidding for your loyalty. But I want to warn you today. Be careful how you pick your masters. There's one fact to consider: You can't serve two of them. You can and will serve only one. As the Scriptures say, you can't serve two masters, for either you will hate the one and love the other, or love the one and hate the other (Matthew 6:24).

How shall we go about determining whose savior we shall serve? First of all, our intelligence should play a major role.

I need a God who can perform miracles, heal the lame and blind—raise the dead! Someday I may find myself in intensive care in Los Angeles. I don't need someone who is in China or Chicago, and can't meet my need because he's not in Los Angeles. My God is so much God that He can hear wherever He is. Intelligence has to play a role in the selection of a god. We need the God who is everlasting, who existed before time came into being. We need that God.

As you choose, you should consider your savior's background. A lot of these pretenders are and were products of their own imagination. Father Divine who swayed so many was nothing but a man of illusions of grandeur. He had a questionable background. Russell Paige is a man of questionable background; E. V. Hill is a man of questionable background. But I know somebody who does have a perfect background.

When you choose a savior you want to know he is going to survive you. If he isn't, what are you going to do when he is dead? We need somebody who is going to be here when the world is on fire. We need someone who is everlasting, who is in total charge. We need a God who has been charged in the fire. We need a God who knows all about and can heal our wounded spirit. We need somebody who has been in the grave and who has conquered death. We need somebody who is now alive, that we can pray to and who will answer our prayers.

Be careful whom you pray to. Be careful whom you give your soul to. Be careful to whom you pledge allegiance.

I have somebody born in Bethlehem, who once walked on this earth but who now sits at the right hand of God. That one is Jesus, Jesus of Nazareth, God's beloved Son, Jesus, my Savior. He's the one I entrusted my life to when I was eleven years old.

He's the one who has never failed me. Since I gave my young heart to Jesus, He has never, never left nor forsaken me.

It all boils down to this. If you're going to pick a savior, the only one to pick is Jesus. He's the Savior worth having. He's the one who will be with you through this life, and in the life to come. He is faithful; He is just. He will never leave nor forsake you.

So when you choose this day your savior—and you must make a choice—choose only Jesus!

Chapter Four

WHEN WAS GOD AT HIS BEST?

"In the beginning God created the heaven and the earth."
—Genesis 1:1

When was God at His best? What greater act could God commit than create the heaven and the earth? That has to be God at His best. I think it was a Russian cosmonaut who declared that there was no heaven, because he had gone up in space, looked out the window, and didn't see one. I remind you, he only went to the backyard.

Our galaxy is considered small when we consider the heavens. Yet, if you start walking from one side of our galaxy to the other, you would be halfway across after a million years. And God created all the heavens. Not only does He have the earth but He has worlds without end. Isn't that exciting?

If there was any such thing as there being an end to what He has, all He would have to do is say, "Come forth." Then He would have more than He already has. We need not question. The act of creating might seem to be God at His best.

Take a look at the earth—all its vastness and majesty. Take a look at its many mysteries. Start, if you please, on the West Coast. Look at its beauty. Even how He took the dry desert and planted exotic cactus plants and made it beautiful. You can follow along the West's coastline and see the beauty of God's creation unsurpassed.

Go to the central states and see the mountains, hills, and lush flatlands, to the South, and to Florida, and see more of God's created beauty.

I called a friend in Florida recently. He's always talking about his land of sunshine, and I believe it was down to about 40 degrees. I said, "Wait a minute," and when I came back to the phone he said, "What were you doing?" I said, "I'm drying off; I've been in the pool." I just wanted to settle this matter about the sunshine in Florida.

Someone says about California, "You have so many earthquakes." I just say, "That's not an earthquake; it's just God walking around."

Look at the beauty of the East Coast. Boston.

The place where my daughter and my two grand-children are freezing to death. Then jump with me over the boundaries into Canada and the beauties and enchantment of that country. Anywhere you want to go there are beauties indescribable. "And God created the heaven and the earth." Including hanging that sun up there that has never needed repair, and putting that moon out there that has never had to have an electrician. So mustn't we conclude that God was at His best when He created the heavens and the earth?

If you want to see Him at His best, look out for His greatness. Fly at night at about 39 or 40,000 feet in the air. As for me, though, I seldom fly at night because I want to help the pilots miss those clouds. God has decorated the night with those things called stars, and there are more of them than grains of sand on the earth. That has to be God at His best.

No, I think not!

AND GOD CREATED HUMANS

Even though those things happen to be pretty good, further on in the first chapter (verse 26) it says, "And God said, Let us make man in our image, after our likeness . . ."

Although I disagree with James Weldon Johnson (he was a poet and not a theologian), he says, "And

God was lonely." About what? Those are traits of mankind, not of our infinite God. He went on to say that God sat down on the riverbank and thought and thought and came up with this solution. Where could a thought come from to God? Whoever would send God a thought IS God!

We often get our human characteristics mixed up with the greatness of God. That's what we would do—we would go and think. But God doesn't have to think. Johnson said that God said to Himself, "Because I'm lonely I'll make me a man." Well, erase all of that—poor theology. God, without thinking and without having to come up with a thought, just made man.

Man with his ability to create great structures. Man who can put a baboon's heart into another man and make it work. Man with the ingenuity to build a great airplane.

Man, who has the ability to invent a medicine that will ignore all other parts of the body, and specifically work on that part for which it was invented. How on earth would my body know, if I take a certain medicine, whether I need it to work on my eye or on my toe?

Man with the ability to think, man with the ability to remember, man with the ability to deal with difficult dilemmas and bring about solutions—but only because God made man. God made man and woman, and gave them abilities to make such things as beautiful music. All this was possible because God made man. God made creatures that can think and produce thoughts and ideas, that can come up with solutions to many problems, because He created them that way. God, without thinking, and not having to come up with a single thought, made man.

I was recently in Joplin, Missouri, which is eight miles from the birthplace of George Washington Carver. I wasn't aware that Carver had the spiritual testimony that he had. I went out to this memorial park dedicated to him. You remember it was George Washington Carver who found 300 different products out of the peanut, including nitroglycerin. This great Negro was a great scientist. One of the things I thought to be interesting was that in his testimony he said, "I never take but one book into my laboratory." When asked what, he said, "The Bible." He also said, "I never invented anything; it was God who revealed it to me."

Even though humanists may try to hide this truth, many great people give credit for their successes to God. All that man is, all that man has created, all that man has done, can be summed up by, "And God created man." Rather than cause a storm by feminists, ". . . and woman."

My first wife went to Glory, and I stayed single for four years, and I finally remarried. Oh bless the

name of the Lord! We are never to be alone, brethren
—keep that in mind.

So let us conclude that it was the God who created the heavens and earth, and God who made man
and woman; surely that was God at His best!

No!

AND GOD PERFORMED MIRACLES

Some will suggest that the many miracles God
wrought and wonders He performed in the Old Tes-
tament, including the deliverance of the children of
Israel from bondage in Egypt, were God at His
greatest and best. Some would suggest that the miracles that Moses and Aaron confronted Pharaoh with,
that must have been God at His best. Pharaoh goes
into his icebox and frogs leap out. He goes to his bed
and it's covered with lice. He goes for a drink of water and it's blood. That must have been God at His
best.

Maybe it was when He made cookies in heaven
and let 'em fall. Maybe it was when He brought water out of a rock, a dry rock. Not just a little water,
but a gushing stream, enough to satisfy the millions
of people, their cattle, their goats, and their sheep.
That had to be God at His best.

No.

That's not our God. He's even better than that!
Praise His name! And speaking of praise. Some of

you ought to take a hymn book to bed with you and sing these precious lines from the beloved hymn "How Great Thou Art," translated into English by Stuart K. Hine:

> *Oh Lord, my God,*
>
> *When I in awesome wonder*
>
> *Consider all the worlds Thy hands have made . . .*
>
> *How great Thou art.*

AND GOD SENT A SAVIOR TO ME

To really see the greatness of God one must take a look at when God looked at man. God made man, man failed, and everything about man failed. How many of you have seen a pretty flower, a pretty rose? If you said yes, you're wrong, for they too suffered from the Fall. Everything went through the Fall!

That's why sometimes you can't even think of your phone number; you've been through the Fall. On the plane recently everyone had a computer but me. All I was thinking about was coming down safely. That's all I ever think of while on a plane. These things all happen because we've been through the Fall. But when God looked at the condition of man, that there is none righteous, that they all are under the condemnation of sin and will perish, and deserve it, this great God who has to be completely just, decided that there was another aspect of His personality —it's called love.

As a matter of fact, if you noticed, I didn't even open my Bible, because when God was at His best was not when He made the heavens and the earth, it was not when He put the sun in place, it was not when He put the moon in place, and it was not when He raised Lazarus from the dead! It wasn't even when He raised Christ from the dead.

GOD HAS DONE MANY THINGS
FOR YOU, BUT I GUARANTEE
YOU RIGHT NOW THAT
IF YOU LOOK OVER IT
YOU WILL JOIN ME AND SAY,
"HE WAS AT HIS BEST
WHEN HE SAVED MY SOUL."

When God was at His best was in Sweet Home Community. Now Sweet Home is eleven miles south of Seguin. Seguin is twenty-seven miles west of San Antonio. You go down the San Antonio/ Houston freeway and you get the Sweet Home cut-off, you turn right, you go down eleven miles to Burland on the highway, and then a dirt road cuts off to your left. That's going where the colored folks live. That's Sweet Home. And it was in Sweet Home when I was eleven years old walking down Grandma Jody's lane that this great big old God who created the heavens and the earth, this great big old God who made man with all of his brilliance, this great big old God who called Lazarus from the dead, this great big old God who made the waters still—He heard my cry.

And He came—this great big old God—dwarfed Himself again and came and entered my heart and saved me. Now, that's when God was at His best. When He saved my soul! A little old country boy, a little old semi-orphan boy with nothing but a two-room log cabin to live in, insignificant to everybody who saw him. They prophesied that he'd never be anything, and I wish they could wake up from the dead now and see me wherever I am. It was when He entered my heart and saved my soul, and I've been saved for fifty-six years! He did a good job. I haven't had to call Him back to repair anything. I'm saved! I don't believe in saved Monday, lost Tuesday. I've been saved! God was at His best! And I want to go further; God is at His best saving souls.

WAS HE AT HIS BEST WITH YOUR SOUL?

God has done many things for you, but I guarantee you right now that if you look over it you will join me and say, "He was at His best when He saved my soul." Even if He gave you good children, gave you a good husband, gave you a good job, gave you a good house—none of that could be better when compared to your ability to say, "I'm saved." And, as John W. Peterson wrote in his song "It Took a Miracle,"

It took a miracle to put the stars in place.

It took a miracle to hang the world in space.

But when He saved my soul,

Cleansed and made me whole,

It took a miracle of love and grace!

That's God at His best.

Many people are using God for everything now. "God give me rain. God give me a job. God give me a husband. God give me a car. God give me a town car. God give me a BMW. God give me this, God give me that." He's fully able to do all of that. But what He is most able to do through His Son Jesus Christ, and by His grace and mercy, is to forgive you of every sin you have committed, to cleanse and make you whole, and to save your soul so that you can rejoice with the others when they sing the lyrics of Jack P. Scholfield's gospel song "Saved, Saved":

Saved by His pow'r divine.
Saved to new life sublime!
Life now is sweet and my joy is complete,
For I'm saved, saved, saved!

Jack P. Scholfield (public domain)

He harmonized justice with love by the sacrifice of His own Son, Jesus. All of us are guilty and worthy of the sentence of death. But God found a way for us to escape the sentence. It is found in John 3:16, "For God so loved the world, that he gave his only begotten son, that whosoever believeth in him should not perish, but have everlasting life."

Maybe you don't know Him as Savior. You know Him as good and kind, but you don't know Him as Savior. You can, you know. Just ask Him to be your Savior. Go ahead. Do it now.

Chapter Five

THE SUNSET
OF THE WICKED

"When I thought to know this, it was too painful for me."
—Psalm 73:16

When I thought about it, it became too painful. The psalmist says that he was thinking about something. He said the more he thought about it, it became too painful for him.

David says, "As I thought of what I was thinking about and what I observed, it became painful. It became painful." Then, he tells us in the third verse what is causing the pain. Psalm 73:3 says, "For I was envious of the foolish, when I saw the prosperity of the wicked."

He said that it was the prosperity of the wicked.

He said that he had observed the wicked, that he had looked at the wicked. He observed that they were indeed wicked. They had no godly reverence. They had no respect for God, nor for God's concerns. They were not loyal to God. They did not study the scrolls, nor did they give any time to the synagogues. Nor did they carry out any of the Law, or the ceremonies of the Law.

They did not call on the name of God. They were proud, boastful, and arrogant. They did not honor God like we do. But David saw that they still prospered. He said he couldn't understand that. He couldn't figure it out. This thought became painful to him. How is it that the wicked can act as if God does not exist, yet prosper? How is it that some people have no reverence, no devotion or dedication to God, and yet prosper? David said it was not as it ought to be. They never even thought about saying, "Thank You, Lord." These wicked ought to be struck down. Their roads ought to be rough. They should not busy themselves with folly.

THE WAY IT OUGHT TO BE

I want to talk about the sunset of the wicked. It ought to be that when men walk away from God they should suffer misery. It ought not be that men can walk around with proud and arrogant attitudes, with take-it-or-leave-it attitudes but still go on and breathe His air, and enjoy His health. David in so many words said, if I were God, I'd fix this thing.

I can say the same thing for me. If you weren't in church on Sunday, I'd fix it so you couldn't breathe. I wouldn't have you out taking care of your yard, cutting your grass, and ignoring my work. You'd have an asthma attack if you skipped church to go yachting and drinking. I'd make your stomach ache. That appears to be right and just.

If God is God, men ought not to be able to run His red lights or ignore His stop signs. To go against His physical and moral laws and regulations and still prosper seems unthinkable to me. But like David I have observed that they prosper. Ain't that somethin'? I have observed that there is a peculiar paradox in this universe of God. God's enemies are permitted to prosper. They do well. David describes them in verse four, "There are no pangs in their death." In other words, they're not always sickly. Their strength is firm. They're not in trouble as other men are.

SUFFERING FOR DOING GOOD

I don't do anything but try to help folks. Yet, at one time in my life I had seventeen lawsuits against me, all resulting from my trying to help folks. Folks who do not try to help others, don't nobody pick on them. The pimp that drives up and down Broadway and Crenshaw, when little boys see him in a nice car they admire him. He's out there spoiling daughters and ruining lives. When he drives by in his El Dorado —they say, "Ah, look at him!" But when a preacher drives by in his Lincoln, "That dang preacher!" When a dope pusher drives up, with his jewelry flashing, and with his bodyguard, we know he's a dope pusher. He drives up in a limousine with a chauffeured car, and everyone says, "He's got it made." But let a preacher put on a new suit, "That dang preacher, done stole some money again."

And David said, "When I thought about this it was too painful for me." The righteous suffer and get sick. The righteous are talked about and lied about. The righteous are held in ridicule. But the wicked prosper. Those people who have no sense of dedication, no sense of love, and boast about it, they're going to ask you what you did on the weekend. Then they're going to make fun of you going to church. They'll say, "I got me a new girlfriend. We slept on the beach and had fun. We drank our margaritas."

The wicked say, "I own the building that you rent, and I don't go to church. I ain't giving no preacher my money. I haven't been sick in five years, and you get a cold every winter." How is it that righteousness seems to be afflicted and wrong seems to have strength?

When David describes it, he says, "They stand out with fatness, they're blessed. They have more than their heart can wish. They are corrupt, and they speak wickedness." There are people who speak out against God and good; they are against righteousness. They come out openly for murder, they push dope, they deal in stolen goods, and David said, "I just can't take it."

He went on to say, "I just got mad walking the streets and seeing arrogance and defiance. I just couldn't take it. Nobody worshiping God, nobody calling on God's name, and he said, "It would have been alright if they'd been suffering, but they were prospering." That's what he couldn't understand.

WHEN I COME TO THE END OF
MY JOURNEY—WHEN MY SUN
GOES DOWN, WHEN IT'S ALL
OVER, WHEN MY WORK ON
EARTH IS DONE—I HAVE GOD
AND THE PLACE HE HAS
PREPARED FOR ME. I HAVE
A GLORIOUS SUNSET.

But then in verse 17 he said, "I went to church. I went into the house of the Lord." He said, "I went to church, and I didn't spend my time whispering or writing notes; I talked with God. I asked God why it was that the wicked prosper and the righteous have such a hard time. Why is it that those who love You, and try to live according to Your Word, are always suffering from one problem or another? And why is it that those who don't seem to care about You have everything?"

WHERE ARE THEY AT SUNSET?

And God said, "You are looking at them at the wrong time. You are looking at wickedness in the morning. It's morning in their lives. Like in nature in the morning the flowers bloom, but when the hot sun starts beating down, they wither and die." Then He said, "They are standing in slippery places. It's slippery where they're standing and at sunset wickedness shall fall."

The sunset and not the sunrise—don't look at man in the sunrise hours. He may be unbridled and ungodly while he's young, but wait until the sun sets. If He isn't trusting in the Savior when the sun goes down, then from those slippery places he shall slip into hell.

My way is rough, but I'm standing on the rock. When I come to the end of my journey—when my sun goes down, when it's all over, when my work on earth is done—I have God and the place He has prepared for me. I have a glorious sunset.

I've seen beautiful flowers come out in the morning, and they're so pretty until about nine o'clock. When the sun hits them, they fold up and by sunset they've fallen away. But then I've seen those old evergreens. In the morning they're green. When the sun hits them, they're green. At noon time, they're green. When the sun goes down, they're green. When the snow falls, they're green. In December and January they're green. In July, they're green. You want to know why? They've got something on the inside, something that I cannot explain.

You know what David finally said? "I decided to stay like I am." He admitted in the second verse, "I almost slipped, I almost decided to be wicked, until I went to church. At church I saw the whole picture."

I challenge you. One day, someday, you're going to come into the sunset of your life. Every moment is bringing you closer to the sunset. I ask you now, what do you want to be like in your sunset days? I ask you now, what good is money when the sun goes down?

I decided a long time ago how I want to leave here. And I'm working on it! I want to leave here weary of life. I don't want to leave here looking back. I want to leave here with my battle done and my victory won. I want to leave here right off the battlefield. So I choose the Savior who will take me right from the battlefield to my eternity in Glory.

David didn't say it, but Paul did, "Know ye not that the unrighteous shall not inherit the kingdom of God?" (1 Corinthians 6:9). The wicked, they won't get there. But the righteous, our Savior will carry us right on home. You talk about envy of the wicked. You ought to see the righteous in Glory. If you think the wicked on earth are doing well, you ought to see the righteous in Glory!

Chapter Six

A HEAVENLY INVITATION

"After this I looked and, behold, a door was opened in heaven;
and the first voice that I heard was, as it were,
of a trumpet talking with me; which said,
Come up here, and I will show thee things
which must be hereafter. And immediately I was
in the Spirit and, behold, a throne was set in heaven,
and one sat on the throne." —Revelation 4:1–2

I want to talk about the predicament of man and a heavenly invitation. Man today is in an awful predicament. First of all, you are standing and beneath you is a fiery hell and so, consider the first plight.

Because we are born in sin, and because we are the offspring of Adam, because we ourselves have sinned and come short of the glory of God, we are all, without salvation, potential residents of hell. There are those who have not yet died who say that there is no hell. But there is one who did die and

went to hell and preached (1 Peter 3:19). But He re-
turned to earth and testified about it, and I'm will-
ing to take His word for it, in finding out whether or
not there is a hell.

I WANT TO REMIND YOU THAT
YOU OUGHT TO CONSIDER
GOING TO HELL AS A BAD
ALTERNATIVE. THERE IS NO
AIR-CONDITIONING IN HELL.
AFTER THE TEMPERATURE
HAS SOARED BEYOND 300
DEGREES FOR ONE THOUSAND
YEARS THERE'LL STILL
BE NO LETUP IN SIGHT.

Hell and heaven are not entrées, like in a cafeteria,
in which you can take a look at and decide whether
you want this one or that. Heaven and hell are true
and real. You must be saved to escape hell and enter
heaven. Hell is a place, a real place. It is logical that
God who is a God of fairness would prepare a place
for those who do not wish to be with Him in heaven.
Therefore He has made it so that anyone who will-
fully and knowingly, eternally wishes not to live with
God will get to live apart from Him in hell. God, in
His infinite fairness, has prepared this alternative.

NO AIR CONDITIONING IN HELL

I've often preached that you can go to hell. But would that I had strength and power sufficient to convince every man and woman to consider the alternative as it is, not as the worshipers of hell and the devil have glamorized. So don't get carried away with all those barbershop and beauty shop discussions. Don't get so loose with the Scriptures that you begin to say, "Well, I don't know, and I don't care."

There are those of you who would not dare to live in a rooming house; you would think it awful if you only had money enough to rent a single room. There are those of you who have a master bedroom, and nobody living in that house but you and your family. Many of you have a family room and a den and all the other conveniences. If it would take all of that for you to be happy on this earth, you'd better not go to hell.

And now I want to remind you that you ought to consider going to hell as a bad alternative. There is no air-conditioning in hell. After the temperature has soared beyond 300 degrees for one thousand years there'll still be no letup in sight. So if heat bothers you, you'd better not go to hell. Because this Bible says it's a place of unthinkable heat. The heat there will never diminish.

Once, when I arrived in Greenville, Mississippi, it was ninety-seven degrees, and eighty-seven degrees at midnight. Heat bothers me, but I was able to go into an air-conditioned lobby, to an air-conditioned room, to an air-conditioned car, to an air-conditioned church. Therefore, I was able to tolerate the heat outside. But in hell, there are no air-conditioned facilities. It is a place of heat.

Even if I thought I could tolerate the heat, I'd have to deal with this fact: Would I dare the risk of going to a place where God is not? I don't wish to wake up any time or place without the presence of God. It is a place where there is no love of God. The love of God does not dwell in hell.

God's love is the explanation for my existence. God's love is the explanation for my welfare. It's the love of God, the grace of God that sustains me. So, to be shut off not for one hour, not for one day, not for one year, but for an eternity in a place where there is no grace of God would be intolerable. The thought that in hell there is no love of God, there is no such thing as God having mercy on me, is beyond comprehension. Just the thought of it is more than I can bear.

REAL SOULS IN A REAL PLACE

Let me assure you that there are souls in hell. There is a false doctrine going around that the grave is hell, and death itself brings to an end of all life, and when you're dead, you're dead.

But the Scripture tells us when Dives (the rich man in Luke 16) died, in hell he lifted up his eyes. Now he could feel the flames. He could remember when he was here on earth. He saw Lazarus on Abraham's bosom. He was so alive that he was praying in hell. But prayers prayed in hell are prayers prayed too late.

You may be here in comfort and convenience. Your job is secure. Your payments are under control. But I ask you right now, if death should strike you down, would you lift your eyes in hell? You might say, "I'm pretty good"; goodness is not what keeps one from hell. All of man's goodness put together can't keep anyone out of hell. There's only one thing that condemns a person to hell, and that is his failure to accept Jesus Christ as Savior and Lord.

The Book reveals that an unbeliever may pray using any other name, but God does not hear or answer that prayer. "In Jesus' name," that's the prayer of faith. If the Muslim asks God to save him and he uses Jesus' name, God will save him. If a Shinto priest uses that name, God will save him. If a Jew wants to reach God, then Jesus' name is the passport to God hearing his prayer.

But in a world of enlightenment, a world that's got the Bible, if a man prays but denies that Jesus is the Christ, even if he falls down on his knees and tries to get to the Father denying that Jesus is the Christ, God will not hear him. You who are dallying with other cults and religions, there is no other name, under heaven, given among men whereby we must be saved—that name is Jesus (Acts 4:12).

Somebody would say, you mean all these other folks will be lost? I mean the Bible says that all these other folks are already lost. "He that believeth not shall be damned" (Mark 16:16). What if they're sincere? The prophets of Baal sincerely called upon their god. These prophets were devout prophets of Baal. They called on Baal all day long (see 1 Kings 18). But the fire didn't fall.

When you pray it's not ceremony, it's not just mouthing pious words. When you pray you want something to fall. You want fire to fall. You want the goalpost to move. You want that blessed assurance that God has heard your prayer. That's why you need to pray God's appointed way.

He has not declared that those who keep the commandments shall not go to hell. He hasn't declared that those who are kind to strangers shall not go to hell. There's only one criterion, and that's when you accept the name of Jesus as your key to entrance.

THE COMPANY IN HELL

Man faces some very bad prospects.

It is impossible to stay where we are, because we're surrounded by an unfriendly world. This is a world that is running out of everything. They're predicting that we will run out of gas, we'll run out of oil, we'll run out of pure water, and we'll run out of pure air. They're saying our grandchildren will have to wear masks every day.

If muggers don't get you, and robbers don't get you, then sickness and sorrow will. This is an unfriendly world. If you don't invite trouble, trouble will knock on your door. If your door is locked it will go under your door. If all these other things don't get you, then time itself will get you. Time will take your hair and leave you bald-headed, time will pluck out your teeth, time will dim your eyes, time will put lumbago in your back, and time will put rheumatism in your legs. It'll finally put you in your grave.

Our path needs to be turned around. Down is the wrong direction. To go down is to end in misery.

When you go to hell, you are in the home of fallen angels. When you go to hell, your neighbors are demons. When you go to hell, sinners are your companions. When you go to hell, there's no such thing as excellence, but rather malice and envy and strife. Violence and misery is what you'll experience. There's no such thing as decency and righteousness in hell. Because God's Son of righteousness does not dwell in hell.

A BETTER DESTINATION

Like the gospel song writer Albert E. Brumley whose song "This World Is Not My Home," I'm choosing to make heaven my home. I'm going to a place that has no death, no sickness, no sorrow. Heaven is my destination.

Every sinner on earth will face God in angry judgment. Every backslider will have to face God by himself. For it's in God's accounting book: Every sin, every dirty deed, every transgression, and everything you should have done but didn't, it's all in the book. If you stand before Him by yourself, God will throw the book at you. He'll say, "Depart from me, ye cursed, I know you not" (Matthew 25:41).

John said, ". . . I looked and, behold, a door was opened in heaven; and the first voice that I heard was, as it were, of a trumpet talking with me; which said, Come up here, and I will show thee things which must be hereafter" (Revelation 4:1). So there it is, true followers, there it is—an open door, and I hear Jesus saying, "Come unto me, all ye that labor and are heavy laden, and I will give you rest" (Matthew 11:28). I hear Jesus say, "Take my yoke upon you, and learn of me; for I am meek and lowly in heart; and ye shall find rest unto your souls" (Matthew 11:29).

Through that open door I hear my Savior say,

"Him that cometh to me I will in no wise cast out" (John 6:37b). From His open door I hear, "He that believes in me shall be saved" (paraphrase, Mark 16:16). From His open door He promises that His Father will hear prayers prayed in His name.

From that open door I shall receive mercy, I shall receive grace, I shall receive forgiveness, and finally I shall receive eternal life all courtesy of my wonderful Savior Jesus Christ.

Chapter Seven

I DON'T WANT TO GO TO HELL

"For God so loved the world, that he gave his only begotten son,
that whosoever believeth in him should not perish,
but have everlasting life." —John 3:16

I'm going to ask you to do the greatest thing that you have ever done: If you have not done so yet, I ask you to accept Jesus Christ as your personal Savior. Not to increase the church membership roll of the Christian churches. But to accept Him in order that you might be saved. I have led many people to Christ whom I have not led to become members of any church. I have many folks that I want to see saved whom I do not particularly want to pastor. I get them saved and recommend the church down the street.

As I mentioned earlier, I accepted Christ as my personal Savior when I was eleven years old. I have not been lost since. I have been saved since then. I was born into the family in such a way that He could never put me out. I'm in there good, bad, or whatever: I'm in there. Whippings and everything else: I'm in there. Like Momma, He takes the board of education and hits my seat of consciousness, but I'm still in there.

IF YOU HAVE NOT DONE SO YET,
I ASK YOU TO ACCEPT JESUS
CHRIST AS YOUR PERSONAL
SAVIOR. NOT TO INCREASE THE
CHURCH MEMBERSHIP ROLL OF
THE CHRISTIAN CHURCHES.
BUT TO ACCEPT HIM IN ORDER
THAT YOU MIGHT BE SAVED.

Why am I glad I accepted Jesus Christ as my Savior? I don't want to go to hell.

Momma taught me that hell is a place. She didn't have a degree in science, and she didn't know anything about the earth and all the workings of the earth, but Momma told me that the Bible said there is such a place as hell. Not a state of mind, not a bad thought, not a dream after you've had some cabbage, but a place called hell.

An old preacher talked about hell when I was a boy. I remember that he said, "Ain't nobody invited to hell. If you go, you go without an invitation. The devil hasn't invited you to go to hell. Jesus says, 'Come to heaven.' It's wrong to go to a place you haven't been invited to."

That old preacher described living a sinful life. He said it was like swinging across hell clinging to a spiderweb. If you haven't more than a spiderweb chance, you'd better get something better than that. I sure needed something better than that!

He talked about hell's blazing fire. I know that that's not the most appealing subject to discuss. Some of you might be intimidated, even insulted by the suggestion that there is an eternal hell. But I want to tell you it is a reality. There's some fire somewhere down there. Now, fire isn't the only thing I dread about hell. But there is some fire down there.

If heaven is a place where all of those who want to be with God go, it's only reasonable, for God is a just God, that He should have a place for those who don't want to be with Him.

There won't be anybody in heaven saying, "I didn't want to go here." No one can just drag you into heaven. Maybe you've been dragged into lots of places, but nobody can drag you into heaven. If you do go to heaven it will be a conscious decision on your part to accept God's provision for those who want to go to heaven. You'll go to heaven because you have willingly and consciously said, "I want to be saved." Because you have accepted Jesus Christ as your personal Savior. That's the only way you're going to make it.

Psalm 9:17 says, "The wicked shall be turned into sheol, and all the nations that forget God." All the Gospels put together say don't fear those who can harm your body, but fear the one who can cast your body and soul into eternal hell.

Oh yes, hell is a place. It's a place where, as we said earlier, there is no love of God. One of the marvels of grace during this age is that the love of God is shed on the just and the unjust, the saved and the unsaved. That's one of the confusing things about this church age. Mercy is just being poured out. Grace is just abounding.

Some people who have not accepted Christ are enjoying the grace and goodness of Christ. As a result they do not see the need of accepting Christ. Because, to be truthful with you, sometimes their arthritis is not as bad as our arthritis. Sometimes they own the building where Christians are renting. Sometimes church folk are catching buses, and sinners are driving by in limousines.

It makes you wonder who's dispensing all these blessings. Looks like they got it all mixed up. Hey, I'm the Christian over here, and this is God's world.

You love God, but you're on a minimum wage. And those who don't care for Him at all are rolling in dough.

If I were God I'd have things so the sinner couldn't enjoy my goodness and not serve me. But God's not like that! He reigns during this period with goodness and mercy. Though He is God, He is standing among those He has chosen, pleading, "Come to Me."

But there'll come a time when those who do not accept Jesus Christ will know no more mercy or grace; they will know only the wrath of God. Because every now and then He lets us in on how He could be. He's holding back His hand right now. Every now and then He just taps us, saying, "Why don't you just act right?"

He wasn't trying to shake up the East Coast with hurricane Hugo. He was just tapping. I think Hugo stood over some parts of South Carolina for thirty-nine minutes, and the devastation was more than we could imagine. Suppose He decided to get rough and tell Hugo, "Swing back there for five hours." In San Francisco, He wasn't trying to be rough; He just let that earth shake for twenty-one seconds. Suppose He got really mad and told the angels, "Go back there and shake that place for three hours." It could be that's all an earthquake is: a bunch of angels jumping up and down. If what happened in twenty-one seconds almost ruined the economy and added taxes onto Californians, what would have happened if he said, "Shake for three hours"? In His grace He didn't do it.

The governor called in his consultants, his engineers, the next morning and asked, "What happened? The bridges were not supposed to collapse. They were built with the understanding that they would hold up in such a disaster." They voted to hire a million-dollar consultant firm to determine what happened. I'm just a country Baptist preacher, but I could tell them for nothing. You just can't withstand God. Build it up to a ten, and He'll send a twelve. Your arms are too short to box with God. When God wants you, He gets you.

GOD'S LOVE IS ALL AROUND . . . TODAY

Sinner, listen! You may not have accepted Christ, but you live in a community where the love of God is all around. Your parents and your friends have shared the love of God. Where you work, you have experienced the love of God. If you've ever been down and somebody helped you, that was the love of God. The motivation of welfare is the love of God. The motivation of charity movements is the love of God.

But what about a world where there is no love of God? I don't want to go to hell. Hell is a place where there is no love of God. I don't want to go anyplace like that.

I had real problems when the Lord took Baby from me, until He came into the room and explained, through His Spirit, that she's on the streets of Glory. I'd preached it a long time—in fact, you can preach about it for your whole life. But He came to my room when my heart was broken, when I was bloody and bleeding, and He assured me that she's on the streets of Glory. Then on Christmas night I walked to the backyard and looked up into a sky that was prettier than it'd ever been, and the stars were bright and twinkling. I looked up and said, "You rascal, it's your first Christmas in Glory." That's the love of God; and I can't imagine facing one day without it.

A LITTLE REST IN THIS WORLD

I don't want to go to hell because it will be a demonstration of the continual wrath of God. I've had my share of sorrows and problems and what have you. But thank God it's not continuous. Because I live in a world where God's mercy gives me a little rest, gives me a little comfort. We've all had our problems. If it's not one thing, it's another. I have a face that's quite bumpy. You can't notice it because of my natural color. It's something I live with, just one thing after another.

There's a lot of folks going around saying that

God makes you rich; He pays your bills. Maybe for them, but I haven't met Him on that level yet. But I know one thing: He saves. He turns your destiny around. He has you bound for Glory. Ain't that good news? I'd say it's the best news!

We are children of tribulation in this world. Because the world doesn't like us. Now if the world doesn't happen to know that you're a Christian, they aren't bothering you. But you better not ever show any evidence that you love Jesus, because if they hated Him, they'll hate us.

HELL HAS NO EXIT

I don't want to go to hell, because there are no exits. You can't take a weekend in hell to see how you like it. If you fool out and go to hell, you're there forever.

Dr. Jack Hyles, former pastor of First Baptist Church in Hammond, Indiana, sent his buses around on Sunday to pick up youngsters for Sunday school. Jack Hyles was quite a fellow. He had around 20,000 in Sunday school. They baptized about a hundred a week; there was just soul winning, soul winning, soul winning. When Jack hired a secretary, he didn't ask how many words you can type, but how many souls do you win? When he hired a janitor, he didn't ask if you knew how to mop, he'd just ask, how many souls do you win?

When we were in Michigan preaching together I asked, "Jack, let me in on why you're so caught up in soul winning. You're on the verge of a fanatic. What's behind all that?"

He said, "One night, I was awakened by this piercing scream from my sister. I ran upstairs to her bedroom, and there she was sweating and in hysterics. I shook her, and I couldn't get her attention, so I had to slap her. I said, 'What's wrong? You had a dream?'

"She said, 'No, no dream.'

"I said, 'You had a nightmare?'

"She said, 'No it was real.'

"I said, 'What happened?'

"She said, 'Jack, I just got back from hell. After a few miles of the glitter and lights and all of that which deceives mankind, there was nothing but desolation. It was a bummed-out situation. It's nothing but desolation and hopelessness. You walk towards the gates of hell knowing that you will never again be free. I got to the gates of hell and the keeper said, "Hold it." I stood outside hell, and I saw people whose faces were twisted and tongues were thick, eyes bulging and hands split—and dropping blood. I said, "Sir, please let some air come in."

"'And he said, "No air in hell."

"'Then I said, "Kind sir, let them have a drink of water."

"'And he said, "No water in hell."

"'Then I said, "If that's true, let 'em die."

"'And he said, "No death in hell."

"'She said, "My God, how long will they suffer?"

"'And he said, "Forever and ever! Hell has no exit and there is no death."'

"She said, 'Just as I turned to leave, he said, "Go back and tell the story." And just as I turned I saw Daddy.'

"And I said, 'Yep, our Daddy is in hell, because he never got around to doing the most important thing. He schooled us, he fed us, but he never got around to saying yes to Jesus Christ.'"

Jack concluded by saying, "I win souls every day so that nobody else's daddy has to go to hell."

I don't want to go to hell. I don't want to be in a place where there are no exits, since I have claustrophobia. I want to be in no place where there is agony of body and spirit. Where there is pain and suffering. Enduring the wrath of God—I don't want it. You can have it if you insist, but I'm going where the wicked cease from troubling, and the weary are at rest. I'm going where there's no more diabetes or cancer or any other physical problem. I'm going where we'll never grow old.

You see, like the old camp meeting song "Just Over in the Glory Land" (written by James W. Acuff) says, "I've a home prepared where the saints abide/

Just over in the glory land." (© 1943, Renewal R. E. Winsett Music Co., Ellis J. Crum, Publishers, Kendallville, IN 46755.) I appreciate the house I have, but it could be taken from me. I appreciate the pulpit I preach from, but it all can disappear. You can be way up one morning and looking for a job the next. But one thing is sure: I ain't going to hell.

Chapter Eight

A SAVIOR WHO OFFERS PEACE

"Therefore, being justified by faith, we have peace with God through our Lord Jesus Christ." —Romans 5:1

I was in Kansas City, Missouri, and I was preaching in a juicy revival. Folks were being saved and we were having a great time shouting, "Amen! Hallelujah!" At the close of a service a girl came to me and said, "Reverend, I have a sister who has joined the Black Panther party, and she is a militant part of it. I want you to pray for her."

And I said, "Why don't you see if she will come to church?"

"Oh, she would never do that!"

I said, "Well, let's pray about it and ask her anyway." And so the closing night I saw—just before I got up to preach—a girl come in and sit in the back row. She acted hostile. Somehow I was just led to believe that was her.

And after I got through preaching she got in line with all the other people, and she came up to me. She said, "Because of my sister I came and I've listened to you for more than an hour and a half. And I want you to know that you said nothing relevant. You said nothing that would bring deliverance to my people. I think you are a fraud. I think you are someone who needs to be done away with!"

Since the other people were trying to shake my hand, I said to her, "Well, why don't you just stand aside a moment and let me get some more kisses and hugs, and I'll deal with you later."

And so she did. And I said, "Now, come in the room here." We went into the room and got on this one-to-one relationship. And I said, "I want to ask you. . . ." Before I could complete my thought she began again to berate me and down the church and condemn our cause—and I just listened to her and prayed. Sometimes that's all you can do.

And then the Lord opened a wide door. She said, "By the way, you tried to get me to accept Christ. You kept beckoning for me and asking me to accept Christ. I saw you."

I said, "Yes, I had you in mind."

She said, "Well, I want to ask you a question."

And I was praying, because I didn't know how much of a Black Panther she was. And then all of a sudden, the Spirit of the Lord brought it out. She said, "If I had accepted Jesus, what would I have now?" That's a door wide open. In other words, what do you have when you have Jesus?

I said, "Now, you asked me, so you must let me answer."

Then she proceeded to try to help me. "Will I have my bills paid for? Will I have a split-level home? Will I have two cars in my garage? Will I have a mink stole? Will Whitey get up off my neck?"

I said to her, "I can't promise all that. Now I don't know too many of us who have Jesus who have all of that. We don't have houses and land, silver and gold where I come from." I have listened to men over the radio that say, "If you send for this cloth, if you just send for this flower, if you'll send for this letter, blessings will be yours. They will just abound. You will have your bills paid." Then they would say, "Now folks, if we don't hear from you we will be forced to go off the air!" And I would think, *It appears to me that some of those handkerchiefs should be kept at their own houses!*

Now, my friend, one of the words that I want to give you before we go on is that accepting Jesus Christ is no immunization against the problems of this world, but I can assure you that He gives us wisdom and patience and faith as we struggle with the normal problems of living. The fact that you do have a split-level, the fact that you do have several cars is no indication that you are closer to the Lord than the one who rides public transportation or even the one who doesn't have the money to ride. But those who are busy across our nation suggesting that God came into this world to give us this world's goods must take another look at the one who came into the world who had nowhere to lay His head. That God has something better than houses and land, silver and gold. That God has something infinitely greater in satisfaction than mink stoles and alligator shoes. He plans to bring something greater than this world's goods.

When I told this young woman that God didn't promise us overflowing earthly goods, she said, "Well, then is He gonna deliver us from our burdens and oppression of the white man?"

"I can't promise that. Because He moves in strange and mysterious ways. And I know how you feel. No one hated white people more than I did until I was a freshman in college. I could have taught Rap Brown and Stokely Carmichael how to do it. Because I was born in Texas. I didn't say the South— I said Texas. I was born amidst hatred and discrimination. I saw all of the evils, and I grew up not only hating white people, but I hated them with what I felt was the sanction of the Holy Ghost. And I really can't even remember when I stopped hating white people. All I do know is that I don't anymore. Because I have a great love that has come through a miraculous birth in Christ."

She said, "Now, rush and tell me."

WHEN YOU HAVE JESUS, YOU HAVE PEACE *WITH* GOD.

So I said, "Well, I have a bunch of them now, and I want you to write them down." And I have twelve things that you get when you get Jesus.

She said, "I'm ready."

A MATTER OF PEACE

What do we have when we have Jesus? The first thing, which I told this young woman comes right from the book of Romans, is: "Therefore, being justified by faith, we have peace with God through our Lord Jesus Christ." Now that's the first thing. When you have Jesus, you have peace *with* God. In light of the fact that He did die, in light of the fact that He was buried, in light of the fact that He was raised again from the dead for our justification, we have something! And that something is: There is therefore now peace with God for those who accept Jesus Christ. Now, that is so mind-blowing!

Financial Peace

Now there are a lot of other places that I'm glad that I have peace with. I remember when I bought my first home. I went to the bank, and I told them that I was a pastor of the second-oldest church in Houston, and it was a distinguished church. I explained that I was a promising pastor and that I wanted to borrow some money. He looked at my credit rating, and he said no. I had no peace at that bank whatsoever. He wouldn't accept my credit, and I didn't like him. So I went to talk to a deacon of our church. I told him I was about to get married, and I had always promised that one day I was going to have my own home. I lived in the projects and in city housing, but I wanted to have my own home.

He said, "Well, Pastor, I think you should have your own home."

"But I went to this bank, and they won't let me have any money."

He said, "Well, that's my bank. How much money do you need?"

"I need $750 for the down payment."

"How much do you have?"

"I have $10."

He went down to the bank and said, "Mr. President, I want my pastor to have $1,000."

The president of the bank responded, "Of course, Brother Douglas!" And I perked up because I thought he had taken another look at my credit rating. "Because of you we will be glad to give it to him."

And he had me sign. And he said, "Brother Douglas, you sign!" I thought that my name, Edward Victor Hill, would be sufficient. But he said, "Brother Douglas, you sign." It was the signature of Brother Douglas that released to me $1,000 for the down payment on my home. His name gave me peace with that bank. Even now, though I've been away from Houston for nineteen years, I can go down to that bank and have peace with that bank. I can now sign without Brother Douglas. They say, "Are you E.V. Hill?" "Yes." "Are you the E.V. Hill who used to be here? OK. What do you want? Sign!" I have peace! And that's marvelous.

Marital Peace

I have peace with my wife. Years ago I remember one morning when she growled at me and accused me of something that I didn't do. So I said to my son, Edward, "Come in here."

And he said, "What is it, Daddy?"

I said, "Tell your momma that I didn't do that."

He said, "No Momma, he didn't."

She said, "Oh Edward, come here! I'm sorry that I accused you falsely!" I had peace with her and I'm glad. It's awful not to have peace with the woman whose cooking you eat.

Peace with the Creator

But, wait a minute! More than with a bank, more than with the board of deacons where I pastor, more than with my wife, I have peace with God. God and I are talking! God is smiling on me! Peace with God! You may have economic peace, political peace. You may have all kinds of peace. Some of you do not have the certainty that you have peace with God! That's who you ought to try to get together with. Get together with Him. He's got you and me in His hands! He's got everything potential and past. He's got your voice, your breath, and your future—everything in His hands. You'd better have peace with God!

I went out to see a member of our church because I had heard she was in much pain and had been suffering. So I went out to have prayer with her. I walked in and she said, "It's so good seeing you, Pastor."

I said to her, "How are you doing?"

She said, "Well. . . ."

I said, "Why don't we pray?"

She said, "May I say something before you pray? Don't ask the Lord to heal me. Don't ask that."

I was shocked. "You don't want me to ask that?"

She said, "Oh no. Just thank Him. Praise Him."

And I said, "Explain that to me. Everyplace else I go, I'm requested to pray for healing of cancer, healing of colds."

She said, "Pastor. I'm almost there, and I don't want to turn around. I'm sick of this world. I'm sick of these needles. I've said good-bye. I'm almost there, and God and I are all right. So let me go." Peace with God.

NOT ONLY CAN YOU HAVE PEACE *WITH* GOD, BUT ONCE YOU GET THIS TRANSCENDING PEACE WITH THE HIGH AND HOLY AND EXALTED GOD, SOMETHING COMES DOWN. IN THE BOOK OF PHILIPPIANS, IT'S CALLED THE PEACE *OF* GOD.

After I told all of this to the hostile young lady who was a member of the Black Panthers, I said, "Now, did you write that down?"

She said, "Yes."

And I said, "Wouldn't you really want to have peace with God?"

She said, "If I thought there was a God and if I thought I would one day meet Him, I would like to be at peace with Him."

I said, "Well write it down. And as you write it down, knock out all of the ifs. He *is,* and you will meet Him."

THE PEACE OF GOD

"Be anxious for nothing, but in everything, by prayer and supplication with thanksgiving, let your requests be made known unto God. And the peace of God, which passeth all understanding, shall keep your hearts and minds through Christ Jesus." —Philippians 4:6–7

Next, I asked this young militant, "Do you have any peace?"

She said, "How can you have peace in a world like this?"

I said, "Aren't you really troubled?"

She said, "I'm troubled on every side. I drink myself to sleep. I take pills to go to sleep. I take pills to wake up. I take pills to pep up, because this world won't let me sleep."

I said, "You can have it! And when you have it, it doesn't mean that you withdraw from the battle. You don't withdraw from the conflict! You rest in the midst of it."

So, the second thing I told her that night is that not only can you have peace *with* God, but once you get this transcending peace with the high and holy and exalted God, something comes down. In the book of Philippians, it's called the peace *of* God. Peace *with* God, then peace *of* God. Paul says the peace *of* God is received once you have peace *with* God. And that comes down and gets all in your head and mind. Peace of God. It gets all in your understanding. And it doesn't stop in your head; it also works on the heart. And not only does it get in your heart; it gets all over you. So that it passes all understanding. And you can get so peaceful in the midst of a storm, in the midst of conflicts, in tragedies and trials until folk who don't know God will claim you're nutty. Peace of God.

I think of my momma serving a hoe cake and molasses and fat meat, bowing her head saying, "Father, we thank You for the blessings we're about to receive": peace of God. An apostle in jail praying: peace of God. Daniel in a lion's den, resting well: peace of God. Shadrach, Meshach, and Abednego saying throw us in: peace of God. The apostle Paul on a ship sinking: peace of God. And it passes all understanding. You can't explain it. No sociologist can understand it. It's something that comes in your heart when you have Jesus.

And my brothers and sisters, I want to slip in a testimony. I have that peace. Yes, I listen to all the newscasts. Yes, I am conscious of the Middle East potential. I have even been in Israel, Lebanon, and Jordan, and I know of the hotness of the Israeli conflict in the Middle East. I know of unemployment. I know they say we're running out of oil, out of gas, out of pure water, out of pure air, out of housing.

Somebody called me a while ago and said, "Hill, I hear you're having trouble." I've been having trouble ever since I've been in this world. I have never known a calm day. I have never known a day when the thunder didn't roll and the lightning didn't flash. When I was in the South I had to be guarded by deacons and trustees with shotguns to preserve my life from the Ku Klux Klan. And I had to be guarded in Los Angeles by policemen even in my own church to preserve my life from black militants. I have never known an uncloudy day! But I've never had a cloudy day when I didn't have the peace of God which passes all understanding.

I have slept with crosses burning. I have turned over and snored when I got calls that a group was on their way to blow up my house. It passes all understanding. You can't figure it out! My wife sometimes gets a little scared. But I have the peace of God.

But Lucie Campbell wrote:

When I should feel so sad,
Why does my heart feel glad?
Why does my soul feel so happy and gay?
When all around me troubles fall,
Yet I'm not worried at all.
King Jesus rolls all burdens away!
Like a king on his throne
I'm never left alone.
He watches o'er me both day and night.
And all that He asks me to do
Is read His Word and be true.
King Jesus rolls all burdens away!

So, I said to this young lady, when you have Jesus you're not only at peace with Him, but you have the peace that He gives to your mind and your heart and your being which passes all understanding. We do not live in a world absent of storms. We do not live in a world absent of problems, headaches, and conflicts. But because the King is on His throne we're never left alone in this world of problems. That's the peace of God.

Chapter Nine

GOOD GIFTS FROM A GOOD SAVIOR

"Every good gift and every perfect gift is from above, and cometh down from the Father of lights, with whom is no variableness, neither shadow of turning." —James 1:17

I asked that young woman, "Don't you need help sometime?"

She said, "Oh preacher, you know I do. I have a child. I'm out of wedlock. Problems are so great."

I said, "I don't want to promise that if you come to Jesus all of that's going to clear up and the father is going to come back and own his child. I don't want to promise you that. You may not ever see him again. But I do promise you that He has done it before. He has cleared up some awful messes in lives just like yours. He's run into some awful wrecks.

He's had some awful fellas on His hands. Samson, Solomon, David and all of the rest of them. And somehow or another when they were at their weakest, He reached out and said, 'Here. boy!'"

THE GOOD GIFT OF DIVINE PROVISION

And so I explained to her that the third thing you have when you have Jesus is my favorite: When you have Jesus you become subject to receive at any moment fantastic, unbelievable, divine supplement. Nobody is sufficient within himself. All of us come to a point where we can just get so far and no further. We all need somebody who is able to put a little rope on the end of our grasp. You can't do it yourself. You need somebody to reach out to help you. And you don't deserve it. And it's not a result of whether or not you prayed all night or whether or not you have more faith than someone else. It doesn't mean He loves you more. It means that every now and then in God's own sovereign will He says, "Here!" He's able to do it. And He does it. Because every now and then you need help.

I told this young girl a little bit about my history: that my mother had five children during the depression, that we had no welfare, and that from the time I was four years old I was raised in a two-room log cabin in Sweet Home by a kind woman I called Momma (who was no kin to me). I told her that

Momma made all of Sweet Home laugh by announcing first that I'd finish high school and second that I'd go to college. I told her how Momma took me down to the Trailway Bus and tied my suitcase with a rope. How she bought my ticket and gave me $5 and said, "Go on to Prairie View. And Momma's gonna be praying for you."

MORE THAN SAVING, MORE THAN SOMETHING WITHIN, MORE THAN THE JOY, WE RECEIVE FROM OUR SAVIOR THE DIRECTION OF AN EXPERIENCED GUIDE.

I told this young woman that I didn't know much about prayer, but I knew Momma did. When I got to Prairie View, I went into the bursar's office, and I stood in line not knowing what I'd do. I told her how Dr. Drew touched me on the shoulder and offered me a four-year scholarship that would pay my room and board, tuition, and give a $35-a-month stipend.

I told her that every now and then when you have Jesus, when you've done all you can do and God knows your heart, He'll say, "Here!"

I asked the girl, "Don't you need somebody to

supplement you? Don't you need somebody to reach down sometime?"

She said, "Yes!"

"Then bring your wounded heart. Tell Him your anguish. Earth has no sorrow that heaven cannot heal when you have Jesus."

THE GOOD GIFT OF GUIDANCE

"The Lord is my shepherd; I shall not want."—Psalm 23:1

More than saving, more than something within, more than the joy, we receive from our Savior the direction of an experienced Guide. This divine guidance is the fourth thing we have when we have Jesus, I told the young woman.

When I was in Africa in 1963, I had heard so much about that continent and I wanted to experience everything that Tarzan said was out there. To my dismay, when I arrived at Robert's Field in Monrovia, we drove up to this Intercontinental Hotel. They had been telling me I was going to eat monkey and snake. The first night the chef was from Georgia; he cooked roast beef. The next morning I got a cab and said, "Take me on into Africa."

He said, "You're already in Africa, my man."

I said, "No. No. Africa."

So he drove about thirty or forty miles on out into the bush and he said, "I don't go no further."

I said, "Well, just stay right here. It may be an hour or two. Just stay right here. I want to walk on into Africa. I want to get it into my soul and in my bones." I walked through the thick and finally a native dropped right in front of me. He had nothing on but just a little string somewhere, and I turned and I ran and I ran and I ran and I ran.

Finally, from sheer exhaustion I fell. He stood over me and in perfect English said, "Sir, you need a guide?"

We have landed on the moon, we have exchanged materials in midair, we have built skyscrapers grand and tall, but still every one of us needs a guide. I was pastor of the Mount Zion Baptist Church and I was a commissioner in Los Angeles. I was well- known and popular. But in Africa, forty miles from Monrovia, three miles from a car, I needed a simple guide. As the guide began to bring me back to where the car was he began to say, "Watch out. Don't step there. Be sure you don't slip into that creek for there are small black poisonous snakes." I had just been running over that path.

If there is anything we know for sure, it is that we are where we are because we are led by unguided men who, like unguided missiles, pose the danger of destroying mankind. We are reaping a crop of lives that have come up without the guidance of a good shepherd. And so man needs a guide. He doesn't know the way. All men need guides. Fortunately, I know one. You can know Him too. He knows the way. And at every point He was tempted like we are.

The people who come to our churches, who are walking on the streets, who are on skid row, who are in mental institutions, are lost and running and exhausted—just like I was in Africa. Some of them just give up. Some of them, out of sheer exhaustion, refuse to go any further. They need to be informed that there is a Guide and there is a Shepherd who looks for people who have lost their way. They need a guide. They need some help.

So, I said to this young lady, "When you have Jesus you have a guide." Jesus, the Good Shepherd, knows the way; in fact, He is the way, truth and life. I said, "I need a guide. The Lord is my Shepherd. The Lord, the Creator of the heavens and earth, is my Shepherd. He is available to shepherd you. He is available to be your protector." And I said to her, "Don't you really need somebody to guide you? Don't you need somebody who is able and who is sufficient to guide you?"

She said, "If there was really any reality to what you are saying, I'd like to have somebody."

One of the habits that I have is running out of gas. It has been embarrassing to me because sometimes I've had distinguished guests in the car. I had Senator Johnson from Atlanta once as a guest, and I was rushing him to the airport. I got to a red light.

And we were already late. And the car grumbled B-R-R-R-R and stopped. Fortunately, there was a gas station right on the other side, so I was able to fill up.

But one of the times when I ran out of gas was on the L.A. to Bakersfield grapevine. And it was midnight. My wife and I were driving into Fresno to have a few days away. The moon was shining. My wife was in my arms, and we were talking. And she was looking beautiful. Down the hill I went, and I attempted to come up the next hill and the car said B-R-R-R-R. And my wife said, "Oh no, Edward. No, you didn't."

I said, "Yes, I did. I just passed a service station, and we are out of gas. And I've got to get out."

She said, "No, no, no! Don't get out. We'll just have to sit here."

I said, "No, I have to get out and flag somebody down."

She said, "No, if you flag somebody down they'll kill us. We're here. This is just it. Let's perish together."

I said, "No, I have to get out. Roll up the window and lock the door. Everything will be fine." I got out and at midnight I was out there trying to flag people down. Then all of a sudden, here comes one of these hot rods. It was all souped up in the back, roaring! Some long-haired fellas rolled up behind me.

And my wife said, "There they are. There they are!"

And the guy got out of his car and came and knocked on the window and said, "What's wrong, Daddy?"

I said, "I'm out of gas."

He said, "Come on, get in my rig. I'll take you down and get it."

She said, "Edward, please don't go. They'll kidnap you."

I said, "I have to go. I'll have to take the chance."

HE WILL NOT ONLY BE YOUR SHEPHERD, BUT HE SAYS IN MATTHEW 10:32: TO THOSE WHO ARE NOT ASHAMED TO OWN HIM, HE WILL NOT BE ASHAMED TO CONFESS "I OWN THEM" BEFORE THE FATHER.

And he put me in his car. We went up and down the hill in one of these rumble seats and we got some gas. I came back, he siphoned some out, he put some in the carburetor, and he cranked it. And he said, "All right, go."

So I said, "Now let me pay you."

"No, no, you don't owe me anything."

"No, I have to pay you. You went over twenty miles."

"No. No."

I said, "Well, why would you do this?"

He said, "My friend and I get our kicks out of finding stupid people like you."

We all need a guide. Men are lost. Some are lost due to their own stupidity. Some are lost due to their own choices. But we who know Jesus know that He gets joy out of finding men wherever they are. No matter the circumstances. Even if they passed up an opportunity to be great and to be noble and wasted their lives. Even if they now sit on the side of roads lost without help. There is a Shepherd who spends His time just driving up and down dark roads and lanes to pick up stupid people. We need a guide.

If you have Jesus, He says, "I know how to lead you into still waters and green pastures. And I know how to create an environment where you can lie down and take your rest."

And so I turned to the young woman and asked, "Wouldn't you like to have this?"

She said, "Yes. If there is such a Shepherd."

THE GOOD GIFT OF ACCEPTANCE BY GOD

"Whosoever, therefore, shall confess me before men, him will I confess also before my Father, who is in heaven."
—Matthew 10:32

Well, there is another thing you have when you have Jesus. He will not only be your Shepherd, but He says in Matthew 10:32: to those who are not ashamed to own Him, He will not be ashamed to confess "I own them" before the Father. This is so dear to me because most of my life I was reared without a father. I always needed somebody to tell other folk, "That's my boy." I needed somebody. When you have Jesus, you have somebody who claims you and owns you, not in the light of who you are, but in spite of who you are. Even in front of the Father who is in heaven, He claims you as His own.

We once had Dr. M.C. Williams, his wife, two children, and sister-in-law as our guests. I took them to dinner at Clifton's cafeteria. I went through the line in a hurry, and I got out of line to tell the cashier I had some guests coming along and I didn't want them to pay. I'd take their tickets. But she said, "But I don't know your guests."

I said, "Well, he's a preacher and his wife will be behind him and two children and then a sister-in-law."

And she said, "I can't operate like that. If they're your guests, you will have to stand here by the cash register and identify them." So I stood there, and finally M.C. came along with a whole lot on his tray.

And I said to the cashier, "That's one of mine."

And in a few minutes his wife came along and I said, "That's one of mine." And then in a few minutes his son and then his daughter and then after a while his sister-in-law came, and I said, "That's another one of mine. That's the last of mine. Add it up." And she added it up and gave it to me. It didn't matter the cost, because they were my guests. I went there prepared to take care of the bill.

JOHN 14 SAYS: I WILL NOT
LEAVE YOU COMFORTLESS.
I WILL SEND YOU SOME HELP.

Life is so situated that we're always getting stuff on our trays that we're not able to pay for. And we need somebody standing at judgment time to tell the cashier, "He's mine." Here he comes with broken promises and broken pledges. Here he comes with sin. He's not fit for the kingdom. But, Jesus says, "Add it up. I'm here, sufficiently able to pay for it. I bled enough on Calvary to pay for it. Whatever it is, add it up. Charge it to My account, and I'm gonna stand here until the last one that was not ashamed to own Me on earth before this perverse generation comes through the line. I'll stand here until the last one comes, and whatever is on his tray, I'm ready to pay for it." When you have Jesus, you have somebody to own you.

Marvin Robinson lost his visa in Khartoum, Sudan. There he was traveling in Khartoum, Sudan, without a visa. But the ambassador's representative vouched for him and told the officers, "Let him through." When you have Jesus, you have an ambassador who's at the right hand of the Father who will vouch for you. And in a world where there is such a search for identification, in a world where there is such a search for being owned and belonging to somebody, we have the glorious privilege of saying to this whole world, Jesus of Nazareth, the Son of God, wishes you to become a part of His own family. And He will not be ashamed to own you as one of His."

When I lived in the segregated South, because of the economics there were a whole lot of privileges that I did not have. There are some I have not enjoyed even now. But I tell you the greatest privilege to be enjoyed has been mine ever since I was eleven years old. And that is that I've had the privilege of singing aloud, "I'm a child of the King!"

THE GOOD GIFT OF COMFORT

"But the Comforter, who is the Holy Spirit, whom the Father will send in my name, he shall teach you all things, and bring all things to your remembrance, whatsoever I have said unto you."—John 14:26

That's not all you have when you have Jesus. When you have Jesus, you have the complete ministry of the Holy Spirit. John 14 says: I will not leave you comfortless. I will send you some help. You have the complete ministry of the Holy Spirit.

When I told her this, the young militant said, "What are you talking about?" And I made it plain to her that before Jesus ascended, He promised that the third person in the Trinity, the Holy Spirit, would come and not just visit us, but live in us. And that He has a ministry of bringing us into the complete likeness of Jesus Christ. He has a ministry of comforting. He has a ministry of guiding. He has a ministry of teaching. He has a ministry of opening our blinded eyes. He has the ministry of giving us directions. He has the ministry of opening our understanding. And this total ministry of the Holy Spirit which is going on right now, making those of us who were unfit to be called children of God fit. And He's working among us, so that the glorious experience and reality of a saved person is that God isn't through with us yet.

The wonderful thing about God is that He has given me enough failures to know that Dr. Hill is not a complete product; His Spirit is still working on me. I'm under construction. You can't be too hard on me! My roof ain't on yet. You have to be careful about judging me as to what I am without considering where I've come from. I am a spiritual being in the hands of the Holy Spirit. And the Holy Spirit, after you have accepted Jesus Christ (without a special invitation), takes up residence in you. He begins a good work, and He never stops. He's working on me.

Years ago I did something very stupid. I wish I hadn't done it. Dr. D.E. King was down to preach for us. And he said, "How are you doing?"

I said, "I'm glad you're here, Dr. King, because I'm about to make an announcement."

And he said, "What you gonna say?"

I said, "I'm about to tell the people that the Lord has fired me."

And he said, "Why?"

And I told him what I had done.

And he said, "That's bad. That was stupid on your part. But now, what does that have to do with God firing you?"

I said, "Well, you know that anybody who would do anything like that, God would have to fire them."

Dr. King said, "Let me see if I can understand what you're saying. Once upon a time God looked out over the earth and saw a bright, clean, unspoiled and untainted, brilliant young fellow named Hill; He was so impressed with Hill that He called him to preach. Later on He discovered some new facts that He was not aware of when He originally called him.

So He has called the council back together, and He is withdrawing the call in the light of new evidence that He didn't have when He first called you."

I said, "You know that isn't true."

He said, "I know the whole thing isn't true!"

I said, "Well, what has happened?"

He said, "God ain't through with you yet! He's working on you. The Holy Spirit is in your life bringing you forward."

That's why Job said, "There are a whole lot of things that I don't understand. I don't understand what has happened to my wealth, what has happened to my children, what has happened to my wife. I don't understand my friends' advice. But one thing I know: when He has tried me, I shall come forth. I'll be all right someday. I'm not in any danger in the meantime."

Like Job's consolation in God's presence, our accepting Jesus Christ starts a whole process known as sanctification—a process of cleaning and smoothing off and filing us down and straightening us out so someday He may present us without fault and with exceeding joy to the Father. There's no threat that can overcome me, because I have a Savior in Jesus Christ. And having that Savior, I have begun this whole business of being constructed in His likeness and image, and I shall be complete someday, because of the ministry of the Holy Spirit.

Chapter Ten

A SAVIOR WHO GIVES US PRIVILEGES

"See how great a love the Father has bestowed upon us, that we should be called children of God; and such we are. For this reason the world does not know us, because it did not know Him. Beloved, now we are the children of God, and it has not appeared as yet what we shall be. We know that, when He appears, we shall be like Him, because we shall see Him just as He is." —1 John 3:1–2 NASB

O ne of the most thrilling things about accepting Jesus Christ is that, behold, now are we sons of God. Now, in our church I would say, "Shout!" This is enough to shout over. This is where all of us ought to be on our feet. Now—right now—are we children of God. That's so unbelievable, that not only does the world not know it, but we don't live like we know it either.

I was preaching with a group of preachers and I said, "Behold, now are we." And I looked around. (I knew them because we grew up together.) And I began to say, "Now Jack, isn't that incredible?" Jack

Rector, Nehemiah, E.V. Hill, the thugs of south Texas? Jack Rector who was so bad that he had the distinction of being kicked out of every school he ever entered; now he is the pastor of the largest church in San Antonio, Texas. Isn't that incredible? That just a few years ago, before the Lord saved him, he was the bad boy in San Antonio. They kicked him out and he landed in Seguin. And he ended up with me—the bad boy in Seguin. And yet now both of us are pastors of churches through the blessed grace of our Lord. We have both repented and accepted Jesus Christ as our Savior, and we have been picked up and dusted off and cleaned up and called. When Jack was called, one holy lady in the city heard and said, "God's hard up these days."

Now are we not just members of the church, not just Christians, not just people who decided to give their lives to Christ but—it has already happened— we are children of God. Reared in a log cabin, brought up in discrimination, knowing all about segregation, knowing all about the trials and tribulations of this world, I am now a son of God. That's thrilling! I may not look like it. But I am. I'm not trying to be. I'm not hoping I'll be. I already am.

In the church where I pastor all of the girls before they kiss a boy must let me see him. They have to walk him past me on Sunday morning. And if I say he's out, then he's gone! So this girl felt she was in love with a Jehovah's Witness. So she told him he would have to go and talk to the pastor. He asked why. She told him, "I'm not going to get serious with anybody who hasn't talked to the pastor." And so, he came in to convert me. They are taught to overwhelm you. They just hit you: Genesis, Mark, Exodus, Matthew, John, Luke, Paul.

So I kept time. And finally when he ran out of steam he said, "What do you think about that?"

"I want equal time. You've talked to me for seventeen minutes."

He said, "All of that stuff about you being saved. None of that makes any sense. Paul said we have to run the race. And at the end of the race you'll be put on a scale and weighed, and if your good deeds outweigh your bad deeds, you'll go up to heaven. And if your bad deeds outweigh your good, you'll go down to hell."

I said, "There's no need of putting me on a scale. If that's how we're going to be determined!"

He said, "Then how do you know you have won? We're in the process of running the race right now!"

I said, "Did you look at that baseball game, the World Series?"

He said, "Yes."

I said, "Do you remember when Reggie Jackson hit that slammer, put it way over the fence, on into the bleachers?"

He said, "Yes."

I said, "Was it a home run?"

"Yes."

I said, "Could anybody put him out?"

"No."

"Well, then why did he run the bases? It's over the fence. It's a home run. But still he had to touch first and second and third and come on home! But he was in no danger. Nobody could throw him out from the bleachers!"

And he said, "What are you saying?"

I said, "On Calvary Jesus put it over the fence. He didn't hit a single. He hit it over the fence. So now I am a son of God, but I still have to run the bases. I'm not in any danger. Nobody's going to throw me out. I'm safe, saved, sanctified. Behold now are we. Isn't that wonderful? That's one of the things my momma could rejoice in. She never made it out of the log cabin until the final years of her life. She never had more than a month's spending money, but she could say, "I'm a child of the King."

Dear reader, let me give you another example, just to be clear. I once hired a young girl to be my secretary. I didn't know who she was other than her name. One day one of my friends came by and said, "Do you know who your secretary is?"

I said, "Of course. That's Natalie Cole."

He said, "But do you know who Natalie Cole is?"

I said, "Of course. She's a very nice young lady. She's here all the time. She works very well. I pay her $2 an hour."

He said, "That's Nat King Cole's daughter."

I said, "What?" So after he left I said, "Come in here, Natalie. Have a seat." I said, "Are you Nat King Cole's daughter?"

"Yes."

I said, "Why didn't you tell me?"

She said, "I didn't know it was required. I just wanted a job."

NOT ONLY AM I A SON OF GOD,
BUT I HAVE BEEN GIVEN
RESPONSIBILITIES TO WORK
IN MY FATHER'S VINEYARD.

I said, "I want to ask you a few more questions. You're the daughter of Nat King Cole. That's the only man my wife ever left me running after—trying to get his autograph. I don't want to get in your business, but I know your daddy was well off and you've been very faithful and I don't pay you very much."

She said, "Yes, my daddy left me something, but I haven't come into it yet. I'm the daughter of Nat Cole. But I haven't come into it yet. I have to be twenty-one. Now, it's there for me and I am his daughter; but I haven't come into it yet."

So, as we sing, "I'm a Child of the King," some of us are sweeping streets, some of us making up beds in hotels, even though now are we sons of God. It doesn't look like it—we haven't come into it yet. But we've got it. Don't worry that we haven't come into all that He has in store for us. The joy of the fact that I'm a son of God does not need to be waited on. I have that now. I can have joy in that my Father who is in heaven recognizes me as His child. This world would have long blown its top and gone to hell if it wasn't for the fact that in this world God has some children. He's holding back His wrath, because He's got some children down here. There's going to be an appointed day when He's gonna call them all home, and when He calls them all home hell's gonna break out in this world. But until then we are the salt of the earth. We are the light of the world. When you have Jesus Christ, when you accept Him as your personal Savior, when you acknowledge Him as your Savior, God adopts you into His own family, and through the process of an adoption He can never disown you.

Within the Oriental system you could disown a natural child but not an adopted child. So I'm a child of the King, because I have been adopted.

HONORED TO WORK FOR OUR FATHER

*"For we are his workmanship, created in Christ Jesus
unto good works, which God hath before ordained that
we should walk in them."*
—Ephesians 2:10

Not only am I a son of God, but I have been giv-
en responsibilities to work in my Father's vineyard.
Now that's exciting. I wonder, has it ever occurred to
you that God, your Father, has permitted you to
work in His kingdom—in His vineyard. My daughter was a student at George Washington University.
When she graduated from law school she wrote me
saying, "Daddy, I'm working in a law firm where
Mr. Haley's brother works." What an honor! When
she finished law school and came to Los Angeles she
was hired by Lobe & Lobe, the third-most prestigious law firm in the state of California. What an
honor!

There are all kinds of honors that people work
for. But those of us who have been called to be
preachers and missionary workers, those of us who
labor in Christian education, those of us who pastor
churches or who are evangelists, has it ever occurred
to you that the honor we have to be coworkers and
laborers in the vineyard of our Lord is infinitely su-
perior to Lobe & Lobe, more prestigious than any
law firm in this world, multiplied by a million

times? God has called us from difficult and sometimes outright sinful places, saved us, owned us, and
made us a part of His team. That's more than playing for the Dodgers, more significant than being the
administrative assistant to the mayor, infinitely more
outstanding than being the right hand to the president. It's the fact that whether or not I'm teaching in
the Sunday school, whether I'm coaching boys how
to become greater young Christians, whether or not
I'm working in Christian education, evangelism, on
street corners, preaching on skid row . . . I'm on
God's team! God has reached way down and selected
us to become team members, working in His vineyard, putting His thing together.

**WHEN YOU ACCEPT JESUS
CHRIST, YOU GET A SEAT
IN HIS ETERNAL KINGDOM.**

Here stands a boy who at one time never believed
he would be able to finish high school, never believed he would rise any further than Sweet Home. I
had no connections, no money, no influence. Born
on the wrong side of the tracks and for many people
with the wrong color skin. And yet, through His
mercy and grace God said, "Come here, and I'm going to put you up somewhere." And when God puts
you up nobody can take you down. Not only am I a

child of God, but God has permitted me to be a workman in His vineyard.

When you go to Greece, soldiers stand outside the palace of the king. Whenever one is selected, it's a great honor to the family. He stands there without blinking an eye. I stood beside one, and he dwarfed me. How much pride he takes in it, how much honor it is to the family: just because one little old king of a little bitty old country selected him to be a guard. And yet my Father, King of Kings, Lord of Lords, everlasting to everlasting, who made the heavens and the earth and all there is, asks me to preach His gospel. Hallelujah! He permits you to play a flute in His orchestra. Hallelujah!

Today and tonight if anybody got a telegram from the president of the United States saying, "I request the honor of your presence tonight at the White House," we'd call a press conference. He's only president of the United States. It's a little old two-hundred-twenty-five-year-old country, that's all. Yet God beckons every man and woman here today, "Come, I request the honor of your presence right now in My throne room." One Thursday morning I got a special delivery from Him when I was eleven years old. I heard the voice of Jesus saying, "Come unto Me and rest." And ever since then I've been waving my testimony and relishing the honor of working in His field.

A PERMANENT SEAT IN GOD'S KINGDOM

"In my Father's house are many mansions: if it were not so, I would have told you. I go to prepare a place for you."
—John 14:2

Next, as I told that young woman who was involved with the Black Panther movement, when you accept Jesus Christ you get a seat in His eternal kingdom. Those whom He hath called and has saved by the name of Jesus Christ, we have a seat in the kingdom.

I once got a telegram asking that I come to Washington. The president of the United States was requesting my presence. I didn't have to worry about any of the arrangements in Washington. All I had to worry about was getting to Washington. When I got there, I just showed up and said, "I'm Edward V. Hill."

They said, "Right this way." And all of a sudden doors were opened. And when we got into this large conference room in the East Wing, there in the middle of the place where we were to have lunch it said, "Edward V. Hill." That was my seat. Nobody could touch it. Nobody could sit there. Nobody could take it from me. I was invited by the president, and his staff made the arrangements. I have, in fact, met six presidents and have been invited to counsel three of them. Yet my seat at their tables was nothing by comparison to the seat Jesus has prepared for me at His table.

Jesus said, in essence, "In My Father's house are many mansions, and I'm going away to set things up for you and arrange your mansion and put your name on it" (John 14:2). We who are believers in Jesus Christ, our way may be rough, our going may get tough, and the scoffers may rise and be determined to send us through persecution. But we are already children of God. We are working in the vineyard of our Lord, and we have the protection of our God. Even angels encamp around us (Psalm 91:11). And when our work on earth is done, when we have finished our course, don't let anybody poke fun at us. Don't let anybody tell us that we're always preaching pie in the sky. We won't let them scoff at our faith. My old grandparents used to sing, "I'm glad that I've got a seat in the kingdom. Isn't that good news!"

So when you have Jesus Christ, you have the best thing on earth. You have the best thing while you go and the best thing when you enter into heaven, for there will be a seat in the kingdom. Praise His holy name.

I love the chorus to the gospel song "When We See Christ," written by Esther Kerr Rusthoi:

It will be worth it all,
When we see Jesus.

Life's trials will seem so small,
When we see Christ.
One glimpse of His dear face
All sorrows will erase
So bravely run the race
'Til we see Christ.

Several years ago I conducted a revival. The revivals I conduct at our church are unique in that you cannot come unless you bring an unchurched person. You can't get into the auditorium unless you have a sinner or a backslider. The pastor does the preaching, but he can't get in to preach unless he has a sinner or backslider with him. When I presented the idea I said, "I'm gonna preach a week."

Everybody said, "Amen! We're going to hear the pastor."

And I said, "You can't get in to hear me unless you bring someone who's unchurched."

That created a problem for all of those who were my leaders, presidents, and chairmen: my influential members. They came in to me and asked me to explain. "I've just explained it. You can't get in unless you have an unsaved person with you."

During that week of preaching, the highest attendance was thirty-two. Sixteen people brought sixteen people. And in five nights we had fifty-nine professions of faith. The amazing thing is that the chairman of my trustee board didn't make it any night. The president of the senior missionary society didn't make it any night. In organized religion the people who are most influential are often those who are not as close or as productive in Christ's work. But in God's kingdom it's different.

There's a lady in our church who's not a member of any of my official leadership groups. She's not president of anything. Her name is Baby Tut. But at this revival Baby Tut, who doesn't lead anything, who isn't an influential member, and who has a name everybody laughs at, every night she had two sinners or backsliders. Every night.

So God has fixed this thing that if you labor as a child of God, if you work hard as a child of God, this world may not recognize you, but you have a seat in the kingdom. Nobody can take it from you. Baby Tut cannot win anything in our church. She doesn't have influence. But she works in a simple, ordinary manner, in a manner that's kind of menial in labor. But when it comes to winning souls, discipling souls, encouraging souls, she's got a seat in the kingdom.

Does Jesus say in Revelation, "Behold I come quickly and I'm going to reward everyone according to who their father was"? No, no. "According to their prestige"? No, no. "According to their works"? Yes!

So fight on, children of God, fight on, soldiers of God. Just a little while to stay here. Soon our earthly work will be done, but we are sons of God and it doesn't yet appear what we shall be. But when we see Jesus we shall be like Him, and He has a seat for us. Not in the White House, not in the mayor's house, but in the kingdom of our God where we shall be forever and ever and ever. Hallelujah!

Chapter Eleven
A SAVIOR WHO LEADS LOVINGLY

"He restoreth my soul: he leadeth me in the paths of righteousness for his name's sake." —Psalm 23:3

I looked that young woman in the eye as I explained the next benefit that comes about when you have Jesus. He provides for each of His followers chosen, selected paths—selected by one who knows the way. I don't know of anything more important than the assurance that there is one who knows the paths that are before us right here and now in this present world. There are so many paths and roads. One could easily devote all of his time and earn a Ph.D. just on naming the many alternatives and paths that are before us.

Life is not as simple as it was when I was in Sweet Home, when the only thing that was before me was to be good or get a whipping. It's more complicated now. And what we're seeing is that young people are being encouraged by parents to choose their own pathways. But when one has Jesus, he has specially selected pathways. He has pathways chosen by one who knows the way. So, then, when we come to a crossroads, followers of Jesus who prevail in their prayers and in their lives are never caught on paths that are uncharted or unchosen and unplanned. We follow chosen paths.

A SAVIOR WHO SHOWS THE WAY

My daughter was a senior in high school at sixteen years old. She graduated from high school at sixteen. She graduated from college at nineteen and law school at twenty-three. All up into high school my daughter had to come to my bed every morning, turn on the lights, and step back so I could see whether she looked like my daughter. And I'd look and say, "Well, I don't agree with that, so change that and then come kiss Daddy."

But when she was sixteen we had a clash. It got so bad that I said, "Come into my office. I don't even want your mother to hear what I'm about to say to you."

After we got over understanding that we loved one another she said something to the effect of, "I don't know how I'm going to be able to stand your dictatorial manner and chauvinistic attitudes for another year."

So I said, "You don't have to stand it another year. I wouldn't want to bore you or burden you for another year. You can move tonight."

It was heartbreaking. At sixteen years old, my daughter and I collided in midair. And she said, "What can we do to work it out? I want to go to college. I need your help. I just can't stand _____. So, let's compromise. What will you do for the next three or four years while I am in school?"

I said, "Here is my compromise. For the next four years you will do what I say, when I say it, the way I say it, as long as I say it. That's the compromise. And in return, I will give you my best. I will give you all that your dad has experienced and all that others whom he knows have experienced. I will support you financially and morally and spiritually. I will give you my best. But I will choose the path."

She stared at me with a degree of resentment; I even saw a tinge of bitterness. Finally she said, "OK."

And I said, "Now, would you mind signing this?" And for the next four years whenever there was a question I said, "Now according to this agreement . . ." At the end of her senior year we went through a

whole lot of things. Had a lot of fun. But I was stern.
Every time she wanted _____ I said, "No, no,
we won't do that." And along about the end of her
senior year she said, "Dad, can I have a conference
with you in the study?" That was always a show-
down when she wanted to meet in the study, behind
closed doors where nobody could hear.

She said, "I'd like to enter another contract with
you."

I said, "No, you're finishing college, and that's all
I had planned for you. I've put enough money away
to help you finish college but nothing beyond that. I
don't plan to spend any more money. You are near-
ing twenty. When you were sixteen or seventeen it
was easier for you to comply with this, but now you
are getting on up where you are going to be grown
and the boys are calling."

She said, "But Dad, I want to enter another contract, and I've written it out."

And I said, "Well, let me read it."

She said, "I will do what you say, when you say it,
how you say it, as long as you say it for the next three
years. In return would you please send me to law
school?"

And I said, "Are you joking? Thirty thousand
dollars? You're going to move to Washington, and
you think that I can't keep account of you and make
you comply."

She said, "Oh no, nobody but the Godfather is any tougher than you. But these four years you don't know what I've been through. But I've learned to love you. And I am so fortunate to have a daddy who knows something about the paths of life. And the only way I'm gonna go to law school is if you take over me for three more years. And I'll wear what you tell me to wear. I'll look like your daughter."

Now she said, "The only thing I wish is that you would be in Washington where I could come every morning and let you look at me."

Three years later, my wife and son and I went to Washington, and we had the privilege of hearing our daughter's name called at the age of twenty-three for finishing law school. After it was over I said, "Was it that tough?"

WHEN YOU HAVE JESUS,

YOU ALSO HAVE A

RESTORER OF THE SOUL.

She said, "What are you talking about? You're going to be my counselor from here out." And I've tried to shoo her away. But the joy of my life was that next Saturday marrying her to an attorney; she did her best to find another chauvinist dictator.

God knows the way. We're not out here without

somebody who knows the way. You may get all caught up with self-awareness. You may get all caught with this counselor and that counselor if you want to. You may even become impressed with yourself, but when you have Jesus, if you'll do it the way He says it, when He says it, how He says it, as long as He says it—you can be assured of choosing the safe path. Call it mindless. That's what my daughter's friends told her when she showed them the contract. Every time a boy she didn't want to go out with approached her, she'd say, "I'm under contract."

My daughter came to me a few years ago and said, "If you try to reach me tonight, I'll be out late."

"It doesn't matter, baby. You're twenty-four now."

She said, "But Dad, when I was in college I had to let you know when I was coming in!"

"But you're not in college. And Dad doesn't walk the floor anymore. You're not a child. Go where you want to go! I believe I have shown you the way and shown you the paths to take."

Chosen paths. Praise God! You know there is a part of the twenty-third Psalm that says, "Goodness and mercy shall follow me all the days of my life" (v. 6). Isn't that beautiful? Because at age eleven I started following Christ, I've always been able to say, "Goodness and mercy have been following me all the days of my life." Everywhere I go. Whatever I've gotten into. When it seemed dark and when there was no way to determine what was good for me next. And I turned to Jesus. I've always had Him say, "This way. This way." And sometimes that way wasn't easy. But nobody told me the road would be easy. For those who have Jesus I'd implore you to teach this to your children so that when they are out there they will know—have chosen paths. When you have Jesus, He knows the way.

A SAVIOR WHO RESTORES YOU

"He restoreth my soul."—Psalm 23:3

When you have Jesus, you also have a restorer of the soul. According to those who know, the number one problem in America today is burnout. People just can't make it anymore. They hurry to bed so they can be the first ones in the bathroom, so they can be the first one to the table, so they can hurry to get to work, so they can hurry and get off, so they can hurry and get a good night's rest. They're completely sick and tired of bedroom, bathroom, table, job. Just burned out.

Manuel Scott once said a preacher told him when he went to preach for him in New York, "Scott, pray for me. Because I know it's wrong. But I hate white folk. I know it's wrong; please pray for me." Scott said that when he went back to preach for him the next year he said, "Scott, double up on your prayers. Because now I don't like black folk either." Just burned out.

We're preaching to many who are burned out. We are working in our offices with many who are burned out. Directors are burned out, organists, deacons, trustees: burned out. And because of position and salary and security and job, many are burned out over the pulpit. Just tired. They need to know that: "He restoreth my soul."

When Marilyn Monroe got burned out she couldn't go any further. When life empties you and when there is no reserve, you do a lot of strange things. You go to false gods and learn how to chant, but it doesn't help. You buy marijuana. For a while you live on the refreshing part of the high and from there you go to coke and from there something heavier. But underneath it all—you are burned out. There is no natural strength, nothing within you, just an empty shell that religion cannot fill and that degrees cannot satisfy. It is something that Mercedes Benz and split-level homes cannot satisfy. And just before suicide, most people cry out, "Is there anyone who can restore my soul? I can buy a new wardrobe. I can buy food. But is there someone who can pick up broken pieces? Is there someone who can restore my soul?"

If there's any one thing that I'm disturbed about, it is how quickly those of us who outwardly seem to be doing all right can jump on a man who is obviously burned out. Such a case was that of a great preacher. I called his church and they said, "He doesn't pastor here anymore."

I said, "Where does he pastor?"

"He doesn't even preach anymore."

I said, "Where does he live?"

"He doesn't even live here anymore."

I said, "Well, tell me about it."

She said, "Well, he committed a sin, and in our church when a pastor commits a sin you have to get rid of him."

I asked, "Would you do me a favor? Where can I find your former pastor?"

She said, "I would not know. But I think there's a man in town who might know."

I finally got his number, and he was in another state. I called him and he said, "Ed? How did you find me?"

I said, "There will be a United Airlines ticket waiting on you Friday evening. I want you to be on that plane, and I'll pick you up at the airport."

He said, "No, Ed. You don't understand. I'm no longer a preacher."

I said, "I didn't even mention that. I said there is an airline ticket at United Airlines. Already paid for—prepaid. And I'll meet you at the airport."

He said, "I lay brick now. I just go to the church and sit up in the balcony. Nobody knows me."

I said, "You still didn't hear what I said. There's an airline ticket. United. It's paid for."

He said, "Well, Ed, if I come it will really only be for talk."

I said, "Well, that's all I'm asking."

And he said, "I'll talk to my wife and see." He called back and said, "I just really can't make it. Maybe some other time."

I said, "There is a ticket. United Airlines. By the way, I remind you that I am older than you are, and in Texas you are taught to obey your elders. There is a ticket at United Airlines."

So he came. When I picked him up I said, "Let's don't talk now. Let's just ride." When we got to the office he said, "I just can't hold it anymore." And he began to cry. And I cried and we cried. And I told the secretary not to bother us. And he cried and he cried. And then I took him on to the hotel, and on Saturday morning I said, "Do you want to ride around and see what the Lord's doing?" I drove him around and he said, "I feel so much better." And I said, "Let's talk. By the way, if you're ready I would like for you to preach in the morning."

He said, "But, Ed, I have explained to you what I did and I have explained to you that I am no longer in the ministry."

And I said, "But we are of different denominations. We are Baptist, and Baptists don't believe in nothing like that. We believe Jesus paid it all. And He has cast our sins from Him. And if you would like to preach in another preacher's pulpit, I'd like for you to preach in mine." And he said, "Ed, I don't think I can make it." So we wrestled all the way up to 11:30 while the choir was singing. And I said, "In another half hour I'm going to present you."

FOR THOSE WHO HAVE JESUS CHRIST, THE BEST IS YET TO COME.

And he preached with power. He preached to the glory of God and sinners repented and people came back and when he got through preaching he fell into my arms. He said, "I can feel something that I haven't felt in a year."

I said, "It's been there all along. You just needed to shake it up a little bit." He moved to Los Angeles and stayed with us and worked with us. And today if any of you are burned out and need a testimony—and thank God for testimonies like that—see me privately and let me tell you about somebody who can tell you, "He restored my soul."

I don't know why, but Sweet Home, where I was raised, is the one place where I can cry. I don't know why. I have not talked to my friend who is a psychia-

trist, but I can't really cry in Mount Zion. Too many
people depend on me to be strong. I seldom cry
around my family. I manage, thank God, not to cry
in the presence of my enemies, for they would cele-
brate. But out where I lived in that two-room log
cabin, every so often (at least once every three years)
I can go out there and cry. I just walk up and down
the roads and cry. And I come back ready for the
fight.

"He restoreth my soul." If you are running on to-
ward burnout, let me tell you today that I have a
Savior who can recharge you. Get some time to
spend alone with God and let Him recharge you. He
restoreth our souls.

A SAVIOR WHO OFFERS ULTIMATE HOPE

*"And I heard a great voice out of heaven saying, Behold,
the tabernacle of God is with men, and he will dwell
with them, and they shall be his people, and God himself shall be with them, and be their God. And God
shall wipe away all tears from their eyes; and there
shall be no more death, neither sorrow, nor crying,
neither shall there be any more pain: for the former
things are passed away."* —Revelation 21:3–4

There is one last thing you have when you have
Jesus—and I told that young woman so. For those
who have Jesus Christ, the best is yet to come. We

need to return to preaching a whole lot about the glory of that which is beyond death. I thank God that I know Jesus Christ to be the one who selects paths, the one who restores my soul—but I join in with the apostle as he speaks to Timothy and says, but there is also something else. We are not only creatures of this world. It is not only the best life to live in this world. It is not only the life where you get hope and divine supplement and salvation and fellowship with God in this world. But don't forget to tell people that the best is yet to come.

The apostle Paul says there is something laid up for us. I don't care that people say that it is all here and there is no other place. There is a place where the wicked cease from troubling and the weary are at rest. There is a place where all of God's children can gather around the welcome table. The best is yet to come if you have Jesus.

The psalmist says that even when we are getting out of here it pays to have Jesus. Because he says, "Though I walk through the valley of the shadow of death, I will fear no evil; for thou art with me" (Psalm 23:4). And the inevitability of all mankind is that we are going to die, unless He comes before we do and we are then among those who are raptured and changed. Until then, every one of us surely is going to die. The signs of death are already in my body. I'm already afflicted with several diseases which remind me every day that I'm going to die. But I thank God that I have Jesus. He not only makes life worth living while I'm living, but He also encourages me by saying "I'm going to walk with you through that most challenging hour."

And then the apostle says that there are laid up for us crowns, rewards. The writer of the book of Revelation describes it as a place of no more sickness and sorrow, no more good-byes. He describes a city —an amazing and beautiful city. I'm not altogether sure of what is laid up for us, but I know that for those who walk with Jesus, the message of the preacher is: The Best is Yet to Come! God has salvation and heaven. God has the Holy Spirit and eternal life. God has joy everlasting.

Those who have Jesus have been promised a new heaven and a new earth. Those who have Jesus have been promised that this old devil will be chained and thrown into the lake of fire. Those who have Jesus have been promised another body, not made with hands but eternal in the heavens. Those who have Jesus have been promised that we'll never grow old. Those who have Jesus will walk together and not get weary. God has yet the best.

I have a home here, but that's not the best. I have a church, a family, but that's not the best. In "Just to Behold His Face," the gospel songwriter Timothy Wright wrote,

Not just to kneel with the angels.
Nor to see loved ones who have gone.
Not just to drink from the fountain
Under the great white throne.
Not for the crown that He giveth
That I'm trying to run this race.
T'will be all that I want up in heaven
Just to behold His face.

I'll bless the hand that guideth.
I'll bless the hand that saves.
I shall not rest till I see Jesus
And take Him by the hand.
Mother, father, sister and brother

And all that have run this race,
Oh what joy will be ours forever,
As we just behold His face!

The best is yet to come!

Chapter Twelve

A TESTIMONY OF JOY

*"But sanctify the Lord God in your hearts,
and be ready always to give an answer
to every man that asketh you a reason of
the hope that is in you, with meekness and fear."*
—1 Peter 3:15

According to this verse, if we have Jesus, we are to be a people of hope. You're supposed to look at us and see hopefulness. Because it says we have a reason for our hope. We're supposed to be a glad crowd. We're supposed to be a joyful crowd.

"I was glad when they said unto me, let us go into the house of the Lord" (Psalm 122:1). You're not supposed to be looking down-and-out. A pastor friend of mine said that he once met one of his members downtown and asked, "How are you?" About an hour later he wished he'd never seen her. Because she poured it out on him.

We are giving a bad impression and a really false representation that we know Jesus when we don't let it show. The world is not supposed to see us all laid out and bound and always on the edge of night, looking for a brighter day.

When the Lord comes into your life, and ushers the Holy Spirit into your life, you are a new creature. A part of this newness is that we drop our sadness. We're supposed to be happy. That's one of the mysteries that make sinners look at us in an unusual way. When sinners prick your heart and stab you in the back, they're waiting on you to break down. And if you really want to run them up a wall, just let them lie on you and hit you and hit you in the back, and turn around and say, "The Lord bless you." If you're easily hurt, folks will keep you in the hospital. Because they enjoy hitting you where it hurts.

By the Holy Spirit we're able to smile in the very presence of the devil himself. As a matter of fact, if you want to run the devil up the wall, and out of your house, rejoice! Have some joy in the house, and he'll run like roaches from Raid. Because he's not ready for the joy of the Lord to be exposed by those who have it.

When you're born-again, when people look at you, they ought to see somebody on his way to heaven. We ought to have a heavenly smile. If you're really born-again, whether or not you feel that way, you smile, because you can't control it. It becomes a part of you, this joy of the Lord. You have joy because your sins have been forgiven. You have joy because you're covered by the blood of the Lamb.

AN INSIDE JOY

Joy is not something you can put on or take off. Some folks find enjoyment in a suit or dress. But if you put it on and take it off enough, it'll get old and lose its enjoyment for you. But our joy is on the inside. What God has done and wants to do for you is not on the outside. Some of you are praying to win the lottery. He didn't come down here to have you win the lottery. He didn't come down here to help you pick out lucky numbers. He came down here to give you a new heart, a new spirit, forgiveness of your sin.

Lots of folks are unhappy because they don't have the house they want. He didn't come down here to give you a house. He didn't come down here to give you a Mercedes Benz. Speaking of that, I call them "Mercy Dez": Lord have mercy on "dez" payments.

When He talked about making us into new creatures, He didn't have a house or a car or a lottery ticket in mind. We've got people running around saying, "I know I'm a Christian, because look what I have." But sinners around the corner just may have so much more. What I have that the world didn't give me is on the inside. I'm even full of joy in the presence of my enemies. They think I'm crazy, because when they've done something wrong to me, I say, "Praise the Lord, brother." Answering their questions, I say, "The Lord knows what you did, and He'll take care of it."

AN OUTSIDE JOY

And so the Scripture says we ought to have hope that's so obvious that people see it. I'm not talking about *invisible* joy. Let folks rejoice in the Lord. Let them pace the floor, run up and down the aisles. Let 'em be noisy.

I remember my first year at Mount Zion. Every time I started preaching and folks got happy, ushers would drag 'em out. Get a little fire started over here, and they'd drag 'em out. Somebody looks like they might shout over here, drag 'em out.

So I went to an usher board meeting and said, "I want to ask you a question. I confess that I'm a little new here. Why do you all drag out folks that seem to be getting a little happy?"

They said, "Oh pastor, we don't want them to disturb your preaching."

I said, "That's very nice and kind of you, but I want you to stop that. How can I get a fire started when every log that starts burning, you drag it out?"

Then I said, "If you really want to help, and you want to take out the one that's disturbing me, then that deacon who's asleep down there, take him out! That's really disturbing me. Here I am preaching my heart out, and he's down there asleep. Take him out, walk him around, and wake him up."

WHAT YOU NEED TO DO
IS WRITE A BOOK,
DOCUMENTING THAT YOU
KNOW THE LORD.
YOU SHOULD START
WITH AN OUTLINE OF
WHAT GOD HAS BROUGHT
YOU THROUGH. . . . THEN
WRITE CHAPTERS FROM THAT
OUTLINE ON WHAT THE LORD
HAS BROUGHT YOU THROUGH.
THEN KEEP IT READY FOR
THOSE WHO ASK YOU.

The joy of the Lord and the hope of us as Christians ought to be obvious. We ought to be just effervescing and overflowing with the joy of the Lord. The Scripture says, to the extent that they're going to ask you a reason for the hope that's in you, "be ready to give them the reason."

DOCUMENTING YOUR FAITH

If you were to go downtown to return something you bought, they'd say, "Where's your receipt, the evidence that you purchased it here?" If someone were to take away your car, to reclaim it you'd have to produce a receipt as a proof of purchase. This is called documentation. Well, one of the reasons many of us don't show hope or have joy is because we have not documented our faith.

What you need to do is write a book, documenting that you know the Lord. You should start with an outline of what God has brought you through. Maybe you've even forgotten what the Lord has brought you through. Then write chapters from that outline on what the Lord has brought you through. Then keep it ready for those who ask you.

There's a lady in my church, who used to shout every Sunday. She'd come running down the stairs ignoring the banister (everyone would fear that she'd fall). But every time she'd get that Holy Spirit joy she'd make it safely down the steps. Then she'd run up and down the aisles—wouldn't bother me at all. Because, first of all, I knew much of her story. I knew what the Lord had done for her. I knew what the Lord was doing for her.

When You Accepted Christ

So, we need to document our faith. We need to write down an outline, beginning with when you accepted Him. You ought to be thoroughly conversant about when you accepted Christ. That should lead it off.

The apostle Paul, every time he got ready to talk, would say, "I was on my way . . ." And every child of God needs to have a remembrance of when he accepted Christ. It may not have been in church or on the Damascus Road. It may not have been down Grandma Yoder's lane like I experienced. But somewhere, if you have been born again, there was a time of conviction. The Holy Ghost convicted you of your *lostness*. If you have never seen yourself as lost, you have never been saved. Because you've got to be lost before you can be saved.

The trouble with a lot of our churches is they've been filled with people who have been in church all of their lives, but they can't remember when they were lost. I thank God I can remember when I was lost. I can remember because the Holy Spirit revealed that I was lost. I was eleven when that same Holy Spirit revealed to me that Jesus is the Christ, the Son of the living God. A part of my personal documentation is when I first found the Lord. That should be the beginning of everybody's story.

Now, if you don't know when you accepted Christ, it may be that you never have accepted Christ. It just may be. Maybe you accepted church membership but you haven't accepted the Lord. Your name may be on the roll of some church, but it may not be in the Lamb's Book of Life. If you never have accepted Christ, you can do so this very moment.

Even a child in Sunday school can say, "I love Jesus and want to be saved." That is the beginning of his or her faith. The doubters should be reminded of Jesus' words, "Permit little children . . . to come unto me . . ." (Matthew 19:14). Both of my children accepted Christ and were baptized when they were five years old. I baptized my grandson when he was five. He came to me and said, "Poppa, I want you to baptize me." I reminded him that his daddy was a preacher, but he said, "No, I want you to baptize me." Then I said, "Well, then, I'll have to know what you believe about Jesus," and he said, "He's my Savior." So I told him that I was ready to baptize him. That boy is saved.

You don't have to go around questioning a child's salvation. Their badness will prove to you that they need a Savior. We've got some little rascals in my church who need to be saved. Their butts need to be whipped, and their souls need to be saved.

We need to quit calling the devilish things that children do "cute." I once saw a mother giving a little child a drink of beer. The little child was acting like he was staggering and everyone was saying, "Isn't that cute?" I told them to stop that. I said, "When he gets older and turns into a drunk, you'll say, 'I don't know where he got it from.'" Little rats don't cut holes; they just follow through where big rats have made the holes.

Evidence of God's Work on Your Heart

Your documentation ought to include where you first found the Lord. Then secondly, your documentation ought to include the work of the Holy Ghost sanctifying you. Because salvation does not include the flesh. There's a song that says, "I looked at my hands and they looked new; I looked at my feet and they did too." But really, you had the same hands and feet after you had accepted Christ. But what happens is the Holy Ghost takes up residence not forty days later, not two years later, but the moment you accept Christ.

There's a teaching that tells you that the Holy Spirit comes into your life at some subsequent time. Now I want to tell you how dangerous that teaching is. What great danger anyone would be if he had accepted Christ without the Holy Ghost being in him. It is the Holy Ghost who surrounds us and teaches us. I would not want to be one minute on earth without the indwelling of the Holy Spirit. It's the Holy Spirit who protects me, guides me, and tells me how to walk. It's the Holy Spirit who warns me when there's danger around. The Holy Spirit immediately begins His work of making me better from the moment I accept Christ.

Now notice, I didn't say I'm perfect, but I am saved. Someone may say, "How can you be saved if you're not perfect?" Yes, I have some bad habits. I have some sins I wish I didn't have. But there's no need of me saying I don't have them, for that would be another sin—I'd be lying. But saved does not mean sinless perfection. Saved means I am covered by the blood of the Lamb. When God looks at me with eyes of mercy, I am clean. You may not see it when you look at me, because you do not have the mind of God.

There's the fellow who may come to church and leave with a long list of condemnation: preacher preached too loud, choir sang too long, folks were too demonstrative. A long list of condemnation. But God looks at us, and He doesn't see anything but the blood. That's my position in Christ.

He has given me a perfect position. He has given me what I have given my child. I can be busy, I can be in conference with somebody, but if my grandson would stumble in, all he'd have to say is, "Poppa." As God's children, all we have to say is, "Abba Father," which interpreted means daddy.

My son has never come into my presence and said, "Dr. Hill, I'd like to speak to you." If he did I'd say, "What's wrong with you, boy?" He has a perfect position. All he has to do is say, "Daddy." Whatever I'm doing, the relationship of a son gives him immediate access. When he says, "Daddy," Daddy drops whatever he is doing and gives him his attention.

The same goes for a mother. I remember when my baby would be crying, and I'd say to my wife, "Why don't you answer?" She'd say, "Ain't nothing wrong with him." And I'd say, "He's crying." She would answer, "Well, that's good, it'll help develop his lungs." But on the other hand, if he reached a certain note she'd hit the floor and fly to his side. When I asked about it, she would say, "There's a cry, and there's a cry." A mother learns early on the difference of a cry and a cry for help. Thank God, our heavenly Father knows when we have an urgent cry, and He knows how to answer it.

I love the lyrics of the gospel song "Love Lifted Me," written by James Rowe (1865–1933), because they talk about God hearing my despairing cry and lifting me out of the raging sea:

> *I was sinking, deep in sin,*
> *Far from the peaceful shore,*
> *Very deeply stained within,*
> *Sinking to rise no more.*

But the Master of the sea
Heard my despairing cry.
From the waters lifted me,
Now safe am I.

The apostle said to be ready to give your reasons for your hope. We need some documented cases. Some folks say that music just made me move. No, no, no. You've got to have something deeper. They've got music down at the nightclub. Even in some churches the musicians tell the people when to swing, and when to clap, when to stand and when to sit. Now, that ain't of the Holy Ghost.

If you've got the Holy Ghost, nobody is going to have to tell you how to respond. It won't stop when church stops; on your way home you'll still rejoice. Even when you get home you'll still feel that joy. You'll start singing in the shower. It can't be cut off —that's the Holy Ghost.

When the Holy Spirit dwells within you, you can't quiet yourself down. Some folks say, "I try to hold it." Don't try to hold it; let it go. They don't hold it at sporting events. Some folks tell me I ought to quiet down at church, but I say, "What I am, God made me. What I have, God gave me. What I know, God taught me. I'm not going to quiet down."

A Book for Others to Read

Whatever happened to you, you need to write it, because some others coming along are going to read it and be strengthened by it. Has anyone ever broken your heart? Have you ever been so broken you didn't want to live? Did the Lord bring you through? You ought to write about it. Did He dry up the tears? Did He mend your broken heart? You ought to write about it. Get ready to tell somebody about it.

You've been through the storm? You've been through the rain? Well, write about it. I've had people so mad at me that they threatened me with a gun, but God was there for me.

You ought to testify. Is He a healer? You need to write it down. Did you get bad news from the doctor, and then the doctor looked at you again, and the trouble was gone? You need to write it down. You ought to write it down: There was a tumor here, and now it's gone. Did He bring you out? Oh, write about it. Sit down and say,

His grace and mercy has brought me through.
Living each moment, because of You.
I want to thank you and praise you too.
Your grace and mercy brought me through.

Be ready, be ready, to give your testimony when they ask you. When they question you, say, "Sit down, I'm glad you asked." Write down the things you know; nobody but God brought you through.

There was a girl in our church who whenever she got a chance would testify, "I was pregnant and the fellow that made me that way took off. I was afraid to tell my folks, but God brought me through." When she gets up and tells it publicly, there are those who say, "You ought not be so open." She replies, "I'm trying to help somebody else."

When you're depressed, take up a pen and write of His goodness to you.

When waves of affliction sweep over your soul,
And when sunlight is hidden from you,
Whenever you're tempted to fret and complain,
Just write of His goodness to you.

"Be ready always to give an answer to every man that asketh you a reason of the hope that is in you."
—1 Peter 3:15

BIOGRAPHICAL SKETCH OF EDWARD VICTOR HILL

Edward Victor Hill was born in Columbus, Texas, on November 10 or 11, 1933. His parents were William and Rosa Hill. He spent his early years in Austin and Sweet Home Community, Seguin, Texas.

He accepted the Lord as his Savior on December 14, 1944, under the preaching of the Reverend Mayes at the Sweet Home Baptist Church. He was baptized in Reverend Rainey's tank and united with the Sweet Home Baptist Church at that time.

In his early youth he went to live with Aaron and Ella Langdon. He worked his way through high school as a hired hand chopping and picking cotton, peanuts, and corn on various farms. He also made the fires for the church he attended.

Hill was active in the church. He was children's and youth choir leader, leader in the youth group, and active in every aspect of the church.

As a student in Sweet Home school, he was involved in sports, public speaking, 4-H, and New Farmers of America. He won many local, district, and state speaking, judging, and essay contests.

He was honored by the state of Texas for his work as a 4-H Club member in soil and water conservation. His efforts won him over seventy-five medals, certificates, and ribbons. His highest honor was raising the Grand Champion Hog of the State Fair of Texas in 1947. He became the first Negro to receive the same price for his hog as did white boys, which was three dollars a pound.

While in junior and senior high school he was president of the Sweet Home student body and president of Area Three New Farmers of America. In addition he was vice president of the State New Farmers of America and president of the regional 4-H Club. He was also president of local, district, and state Baptist youth organizations.

Upon graduation from Sweet Home High School, he was awarded a four-year Jessie Jones Scholarship to attend the Prairie View (Texas) College, which he entered in the fall of 1951, majoring in Agronomy. He was class reporter of his freshman class. In addition, he was president of the New Farmer's class and leader of the National Baptist Student Union. He was preacher for the Tuesday night prayer meeting that averaged 1,100 students each week.

He received his call to preach in 1951 and soon after was licensed. He was ordained as a Baptist minister on December 29, 1954, by the Greater Mount Zion Missionary Baptist Church in Austin, Texas, of which Reverend J. H. Washington was pastor. He received his first call to pastor the Friendly Will Missionary Baptist Church in Austin, Texas, in 1954. He was also director of youth of the General Baptist Convention in Texas. Listed among "Who's Who in American Colleges and Universities in America," he graduated in 1955 among the top ten.

In 1955 he became pastor of the Mount Corinth Missionary Baptist Church of Houston, one of Houston's oldest and most prestigious congregations. He was twenty-one and single. But that soon changed when he married Jane Edna Coruthers, daughter of Dr. John and Susie Coruthers, in Prairie View Texas on August 29, 1955.

Through his pastorate there he led the congregation into becoming one of the most influential congregations in the state. The membership grew from 214 to 1,100 active members in six years. The church was known to have one of the largest youth groups in America. Through his leadership his church came into full participation in social, political, and civic endeavors. When the NAACP was outlawed in Texas, through Mount Corinth, Pastor Hill organized the Freedom Fund of Texas.

While pastoring Mount Corinth, Pastor Hill was an original board member of the Southern Christian Leadership Conference and nominated Dr. Martin Luther King as president.

Besides his office as pastor, he also served on local, statewide, and national boards. He was on the executive committee of the Baptist World Youth Conference in 1956. He served as a board member of the NAACP of Houston and the Negro Chamber of Commerce of Houston. Hill organized and was executive director of the Master Handicapped Workers of Texas, and was an active Democrat. He was an activist in more causes than there is room to enumerate. Worthy of mention is the awarding of an honorary Doctor of Law degree by Union Baptist Theological Seminary of Houston.

On the first Sunday in 1961, Dr. Hill became pastor of the historic Mount Zion Missionary Baptist Church of Los Angeles, one of the oldest and most influential churches. The church was organized in 1892 with the peaceful exodus from the Second Baptist Church, to better serve the interests of the Southern constituents. During his tenure as pastor he has inaugurated many changes. First he suspended all the organizations and officers. Then he methodically reorganized the structure of the church based on biblical principles. When he arrived the church was facing foreclosure. Within six months every note was paid. There were also $151,000 of lawsuits pending, which he settled within three months. The church property was refurbished and two additional lots were purchased. The complete remodeling of the sanctuary was accomplished at a cost of $200,000, a great sum at that time. It is well-known as a missionary giving church donating thousands of dollars to various missions projects throughout the world every year.

Dr. Hill and his wife, during the thirty-two years of their marriage, raised two children, Norva Rose Hill (Kennard) and Edward Victor Hill II. They also have five grandsons and one granddaughter.

In 1987 Dr. Hill's beloved wife, Jane Edna, whom he called Baby, went home to be with the Lord. After four years of being alone, Hill was re-married to LaDean Donald on March 7, 1992.

Throughout the years Pastor Hill has preached the uncompromising gospel of Jesus Christ and maintains a high level of gospel presented from the pulpit of the Mount Zion Baptist Church. He has received over 10,000 people who have come down the aisles committing or recommitting themselves to Christ. He has baptized into the fellowship of the church over 3,000 people who have confessed the Lord as Savior. Through his evangelistic fervor he has seen over 25,000 people throughout the United States accept Christ as their Savior.

Dr. Hill has maintained a strenuous schedule of preaching and teaching for conventions, universities, colleges, seminaries, Bible conferences, local churches, and city-wide revivals throughout the world. He receives an average of 200 invitations per year which keep him out of the pulpit of Mount Zion approximately twenty-four Sundays every year.

To recount all of his accomplishments and involvements in the religious and secular fields would take more pages than this book could hold. Dr. Edward Victor Hill has distinguished himself as a warrior of the faith and has been used of God in remarkable ways.

STEPS TO PEACE WITH GOD

1. RECOGNIZE GOD'S PLAN—PEACE AND LIFE

The message you have read in this book stresses that God loves you and wants you to experience His peace and life.

The BIBLE says . . . *"For God loved the world so much that He gave His only Son, so that everyone who believes in Him may not die but have eternal life." John 3:16*

2. REALIZE OUR PROBLEM—SEPARATION

People choose to disobey God and go their own way. This results in separation from God.

The BIBLE says . . . *"Everyone has sinned and is far away from God's saving presence." Romans 3:23*

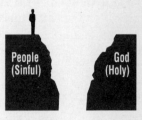

3. RESPOND TO GOD'S REMEDY—CROSS OF CHRIST

God sent His Son to bridge the gap. Christ did this by paying the penalty of our sins when He died on the cross and rose from the grave.

The BIBLE says . . . *"But God has shown us how much He loves us—it was while we were still sinners that Christ died for us!" Romans 5:8*

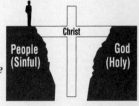

4. RECEIVE GOD'S SON—LORD AND SAVIOR

You cross the bridge into God's family when you ask Christ to come into your life.

The BIBLE says . . . *"Some, however, did receive Him and believed in Him; so He gave them the right to become God's children." John 1:12*

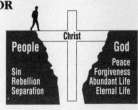

THE INVITATION IS TO:
REPENT (turn from your sins) and by faith RECEIVE Jesus Christ into your heart and life and follow Him in obedience as your Lord and Savior.

PRAYER OF COMMITMENT
"Lord Jesus, I know I am a sinner. I believe You died for my sins. Right now, I turn from my sins and open the door of my heart and life. I receive You as my personal Lord and Savior. Thank You for saving me now. Amen."

If you want further help in the decision you have made, write to:
Billy Graham Evangelistic Association, P.O. Box 779, Minneapolis, MN 55440-0779

A SAVIOR WORTH HAVING

Key of C
Copyright 2002
by ROSETTA MINES

Chorus
How righteous is our God
Holy is our God
Faithful is our God
He's a Savior worth having
How righteous is our God
Holy is our God
Faithful is our God ever true. Oh (repeat)

Verse 1
It's not for fame or fortune
Why we praise Your name
It's not wealth or treasures
That this world affords
But it is the joy unspeakable and full of glory
Why we magnify Your holy name (Chorus)

Verse 2
He's the joy of my salvation
He's my shelter from the storm
He's beside me, always to guide me
He keeps me from all harm
For He is Christ my Savior
He's God and God alone
And I magnify His holy name

Faithful is our God ever true
Faithful is our God ever true
Faithful is our God ever true

Faithful is our God
Faithful is our God
Faithful is our God ever true